Athlete's Cookbook

USA Gymnastics

Masters Press

A Division of Howard W. Sams & Co.
A Bell Atlantic Company

Published by Masters Press (A Division of Howard W. Sams &
     Company, A Bell Atlantic Company)
2647 Waterfront Pkwy E. Dr, Suite 300,
Indianapolis, IN 46214

Printed in the United States of America.

10   9   8   7   6   5   4   3   2   1

Library of Congress Cataloging-in-Publication Data

Athlete's cookbook / USA gymnastics.
            p. cm.
      ISBN 1-57028-052-5 (pbk)
            1. Athletes — Nutrition. 2. Cookery. 3. Gymnasts — Nu-
            trition.
      I. USA gymnastics.
      TX361.A8A75   1995   95-40462
      613.2'024796--dc20   CIP

Contents

Credits

Editor: Michelle Dusserre, R.D.

Contributing Editors:

    Dan Benardot, Ph.D., R.D., L.D.

    Nancy Marshall, Olympian, USA Gymnastics Vice Chair for Women

    Donna Evans, M.S., R.D.

In-house Editor: Heather Seal

Cover Design: Kelly Ternet

Diagrams: Suzanne Lincoln

Proofreader: Pat Brady

Special thanks to Matt Farrell

INTRODUCTION

Gymnastics. It is a sport that has grown in the last 20 years to become the most popular Olympic spectator sport. The world watches closely to see who will be crowned the next Olympic champion. But a difficult road lies ahead of anyone who desires to pursue excellence in this sport. Whether it be a state competition or a World or Olympic Championship, that road demands sacrifice. We choose the best gym clubs to attend, and the best coaches to train us. We spend time with our coaches to plan a schedule that can both handle our training as well as school. Our coaches develop plans for summer training, in-season training, and conditioning. All of these decisions are made from past experience and from the expertise of the coaching staff. Everything is in place for an environment that will help us achieve our gymnastics goals.

However, I've seen many gymnasts, myself included, unable to keep up with this schedule. Lack of energy is the main complaint. I have asked some of the college women I've coached about their day leading up to this energy problem. The day usually has started out with not enough sleep, college exams and not enough time to eat a good meal. And yet they wonder why they can't finish practice. Looking back I am amazed at how I ate when I was competing, and I really wonder how I was able to go on for weeks and months by eating a diet that was low in carbohydrates and low in calories.

Once I became interested in nutrition, I realized how I could get the most out of what I ate. It started to make sense, and many of the myths that I had about food were replaced by solid facts about carbohydrates, fats, proteins, vitamins and minerals.

By reading this book, gymnasts can hopefully learn earlier than I did about the importance of eating right and how it can benefit your training. It is my hope that with this information nutrition and healthy eating will become part of your training plan for a long and successful gymnastics career.

Michelle Dusserre
1984 Olympian

CHAPTER 1
Nutrition Basics For Backflips

For the human body to survive, it needs the necessities of life: water, shelter, warmth, clothing and food. However, most people look at food as more than just a part of this basic list. Eating is more than fuel for our body. It is Thanksgiving dinner, a summer picnic, a hot dog at the ballpark. One of the most important parts of culture in any society centers around food. Companies spend millions of dollars developing new food products, and billions of dollars to advertise these items on TV, radio and billboards.

Unfortunately, Americans don't have the time or the patience to strip food down to what it really is: the means of providing nourishment and energy to our bodies. Fancy wrappers, hip slogans and high price tags all mask food's true purpose: eating for life.

Eating is not one of those activities we can choose to live without. You may have heard of the comparison made between the human body and a car. Both need fuel, which is the energy that allows both the car and our bodies to function. However, fuel to our bodies must never stop because our bodies are always "turned on." A car can sit in a driveway for months without needing fuel, but once the car is turned on, it needs fuel to keep going. Nourishment means providing those items that are needed for life and growth. Nourishment to our bodies is something that must be done at least three times every day. The human body needs fuel on a constant basis, and we cannot ignore this.

NUTRIENTS

Our bodies run on many different types of fuels. There are six major nutrients that we must consume (or eat) to survive. They are:

-Vitamins   -Water   -Protein
-Minerals   -Fat   -Carbohydrates

Only carbohydrates, protein and fats give us energy. This energy is better known as calories. Calories are a measure of food energy, but we need vitamins and minerals to help us convert this food energy to the energy our body needs. Water is needed to provide the right environment to do this.

CARBOHYDRATES

Just as there are picky eaters, our body is picky about the order in which it uses these different types of fuels. Carbohydrates are the energy of choice, and they are found in either a simple or complex form. Simple carbohydrates, or sugars, are found in vitamin-rich foods such as fruits and vegetables, and in nutrient-poor foods such as cakes, cookies and candy.

Complex carbohydrates, or starches, are called that because they are sugar molecules that are packed together in a small space. Foods that contain complex carbohydrates pack and carry more carbohydrate molecules than foods with simple carbohydrates. This is better because the energy that you get from complex carbohydrates lasts longer. Complex carbohydrates are usually good sources of vitamins and minerals as well, and can be found in such foods as breads, starchy vegetables (like potatoes), and beans.

When eaten, carbohydrates are metabolized to glucose. To metabolize means to break down elements, such as carbohydrates, and to release energy that will be available for many functions in our body. Glucose is like a burning flame, so to speak, and is the first link to making energy. Glucose is constantly searching for something to combine with, so it can ignite and release its energy. When our blood contains enough glucose, extra glucose that is not needed is converted to glycogen, a storage form of glucose, and stored for use later.

If the glucose in our blood is low, the glycogen is pulled out of storage (from either our muscles or the liver) and converted back to glucose. Our bodies continuously send out signals for needing energy. ATP is something that picks up these signals. ATP is made from the calories we eat, and it is like an unlit sparkler. Once ATP and glucose cross their signals, they combine with each other; the sparkler is lit and the energy is available for the body to use.[1] If you don't feed your body enough carbohydrates, it will first use the stored glycogen as energy. If there is no stored glycogen to use, the body, which still needs to make this energy, goes to protein and fat as an energy source.

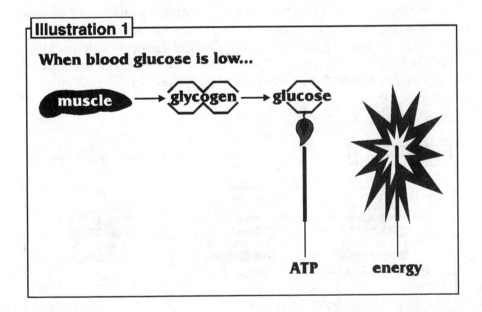

Illustration 1

When blood glucose is low...

muscle → glycogen → glucose

ATP   energy

PROTEIN

Protein's main purpose is to rebuild and repair tissue. If the diet is low in carbohydrates, the body will be forced to burn protein for energy, pulling it away from its job of repairing. Proteins can be used in the same way that carbohydrates are used, and they can keep blood glucose levels normal. Proteins also make up enzymes, which help reactions in our body happen. Some of these reactions include managing hormones (chemical reactions) and keeping body fluids in balance. When proteins are burned as fuel, however, they leave behind bad waste products that the body must dispose.

FATS

Fats are another form of energy that the body can use. They are also important for the metabolism of vitamins A, D, E, and K, maintaining body temperature and cushioning many of the important organs like the heart. Fats work with oxygen to produce even more energy than the carbohydrates or protein can produce. This is because fats provide more than two times the amount of calories per gram than carbohydrates or protein.

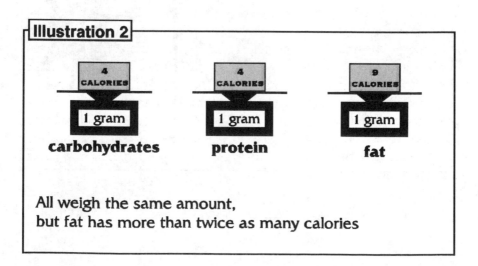

Illustration 2

4 CALORIES	4 CALORIES	9 CALORIES
1 gram	1 gram	1 gram
carbohydrates	**protein**	**fat**

All weigh the same amount,
but fat has more than twice as many calories

Fats are not used in the same way that carbohydrates and proteins are used. They use a different system to supply energy. Use of fats without the help of carbohydrates can result in a buildup called ketones. Normally, when fat is used for energy it needs carbohydrate to be completely broken down. In ketosis, fat is broken down incompletely, leaving behind toxic (poisonous) ketones which, over time, can be damaging to the liver.

ALL TOGETHER NOW...

The United States Department of Agriculture (USDA) recommends that the healthy adult should get 10% of their calories from simple carbohydrates, 48% of their calories from complex carbohydrates, 12% of their calories from protein and 30% or less of their calories from fat. A typical American diet contains about 40-45% fat,[2] an unhealthy level of fat for anyone. But the typical American is not like the typical athlete, because they don't train numerous hours a week and they don't demand the physical stress that a sport like gymnastics can put on the body.

Athletes' energy needs are special. Carbohydrates, proteins and fats all provide energy, but the athletes need the calories they eat to be in the form that they will use most often for their specific sport. Athletes fall into many different categories themselves. Different sports have different physical demands. A marathon runner has a different physical demand than a gymnast. Another example can be used between a weightlifter and a triathlete. Both need most of their calories from carbohydrates (the first choice of energy that our body prefers). The weightlifter uses this energy in quick spurts, and he musters all of his energy for one lift which lasts maybe ten seconds. The triathlete, however, uses this energy over a long period of time, for sometimes up to nine or ten hours. These examples are extreme, but they are a good way to show the differences between sports and their energy needs.

Triathlete   Weightlifter

O-2 USE OXYGEN

Anaerobic means the process of burning energy without oxygen. When the body and muscles need energy, they send a signal to where that energy is stored. If the energy is needed for a very explosive activity (for example, a vault), the stored energy (glycogen) can be used without oxygen.

It takes about two minutes for the body to switch gears and start using oxygen for burning energy. Once oxygen can reach the muscles they can use both glucose and fat for energy. This is called aerobic energy. Both anaerobic gymnasts and aerobic runners use glycogen for energy. The runner, however, uses oxygen during his exercise. Because runners are aerobic athletes, they burn more fat than gymnasts.

With this information, it is easier to put different types of sports into different categories.

Table 1: Sports and Their Energy Needs

- Endurance: Swimming, Rowing, Running, Cycling, Skiing
- Strength: Body Building (male and female), Weightlifting, Gymnastics, Judo
- Team Sport: Water Polo, Soccer, Hockey, Volleyball, Handball

Adapted from Nationwide Survey on Nutrition Habits in Elite Athletes Part I. Energy, Carbohydrates, Protein and Fat Intake, by van Erp-Baart AMJ, Saris WHM, Binkhorst RA, Vos JA, and Elvers JWH. International Journal of Sports Medicine, 10, p. S4, 1989. Copyright 1989 by IJSM. Reprinted with permission.

Gymnastics falls into the same category as weightlifting because it requires quick spurts of energy for a short length of time (no more than 30-90 seconds). The aerobic system needs at least two minutes (or 120 seconds) to switch from an anaerobic to an aerobic process.[2] A gymnastics routine does not last long enough for oxygen to reach the system to burn fat as fuel.

Many gymnasts claim, "I work out 5 to 7 hours a day, so shouldn't I be burning fat?" Though it may seem like it, gymnasts do not burn a great amount of fat. The stop-and-go spurts of performing gymnastics routines and the rest in between only signals the body to use its quick, anaerobic energy source (carbohydrates). The body is never given a chance to use any other fuel source.

THE RIGHT STUFF

So, what is the magic answer to all of this for gymnasts? The key is to give your body the most of what it needs and as often as needed. Long practice sessions of 5 to 7 hours will drain the body of important glycogen stores. Snacks during practice will help keep glycogen levels from going empty, and will also keep the mind alert and functioning through the end of practice. A diet made up of at least 62-65% carbohydrates (both complex and simple), 15-18% protein, and 20% or less fat meets the energy needs of the athlete in the most sensible way. The carbohydrate level gives the gymnast the important fuel needed for the anaerobic nature of gymnastics. The amount of protein provided is enough for tissue repair and the important tasks of protein. The level of fat is a reasonable level achieved in a well-rounded, well-balanced meal plan.

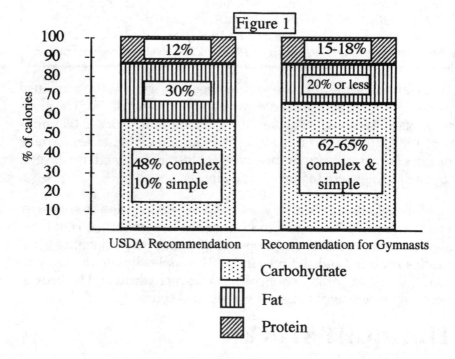

Figure 1

CARBS GALORE

There are many endurance, or aerobic, athletes who eat a diet that is very, very high in carbohydrates right before the event in hopes of filling their carbohydrate stores to the maximum. This is called carbohydrate loading. It is basically done by eating a normal amount of carbohydrate while training to exhaustion the week before a big competition, and then eating a very high carbohydrate diet while resting for three days immediately before the competition. If done correctly, this may prevent the athlete from "hitting the wall" (completely running out of glycogen) toward the end of the event. Many endurance athletes do this because their competition requires from 2-4 hours of continuous, intense exercise. Because gymnastics is a stop-and-go sport, carbohydrate loading is not necessary. A regular meal before the meet and a snack during the meet will provide gymnasts with what they need for a peak performance.

Figure 2
How does fat figure? How do you know if you are eating a diet that is 25% fat? Look at the label of the food you are eating. To know that you are eating a diet that is 25% fat or less, the food shouldn't have more than 2.5 grams of fat per 100 calories. Guide: 2.0 grams of fat per 100 calories 4.0 grams of fat per 200 calories 6.0 grams of fat per 300 calories.
Example: An item that contains 300 calories and 10 grams of fat is higher in fat than our guide indicates as 20% fat. This is an example of how to figure out the percentage of fat in each food eaten. Remember, this is a guide, and it does not mean that every single food eaten must be exact to this amount of fat. Some foods will be higher in fat, and others will be lower. The goal is to achieve a diet that is 20% fat, 62-65% carbohydrates, and 15-18% protein over a period of time. Every day will be different from the next, but a diet with 20% fat over time (week to week) is the ultimate goal.

VITAMIN SUPPLEMENTS: WORTH THEIR WEIGHT IN GOLD?

As the saying goes, you can never have too much of a good thing. So you walk by the local health food store and see advertisements for vitamin and mineral supplements that are ten times the RDA. The salesperson sounds convincing when he says that you need this supplement because of your athletic nature.

Your first question should be, "What is my Recommended Dietary Allowance?" Secondly, you should ask, "Do I need more than what is recommended?"

You can't have too much of a good thing, right? Wrong! Your body only uses what it needs, and what it doesn't need it must get rid of. Taking a supplement that provides many times more than what your body needs can be dangerous. Supplements can be safe if they are used wisely. A general multivitamin and mineral supplement that provides just 100% of the Recommended Dietary Allowance (or RDA, the amount of nutrients considered adequate but safe for maintaining health) can help make up for a day that you may not eat 100% of the RDA. However, they should not be used to correct for a bad diet day-in and day-out. The best source of vitamins and minerals that you can hope for is from whole food that has had minimum processing (whole wheat bread, raw fruits and vegetables, fresh meats and milk).

Processed or refined foods are foods that usually have had the vitamins removed during the processing, and replaced later on while the processing is still taking place. Many vitamins and minerals that are removed from the raw food are not put back in. All of the major vitamins and minerals are usually replaced, but it's the trace minerals (those minerals that we only need in very small amounts) that are usually not replaced.

If we only need a small amount of trace minerals, should we be concerned? It should be a concern for someone who eats a diet that contains a high amount of refined foods. The more refined or processed foods eaten, the less of a chance those trace minerals will be included in the diet. Trace minerals such as chromium, zinc, fluoride and manganese are not usually replaced back into the food, but they have important roles in our health. Chromium is important for controlling our blood glucose (2). Even though we only need a very small amount, a lack of chromium could make the difference in good blood glucose control. If you do eat a diet rich in whole fruits, vegetables, grains, lean meats and dairy products, getting your daily requirement of trace minerals shouldn't be a problem.

The most important idea in all of this is that foods contain many nutrients (some that may not have even been discovered yet), and the best way to make sure that we get everything we need is to eat a wide variety of foods. It's just that simple!

Listed in Table 2 are the amounts of vitamins and minerals we need in the amounts that are suggested by the Food and Nutrition Board. The RDA's are amounts that allow for more than the needs of the average person. They are a safe but adequate amount, meaning that they are enough to ensure good health, but not too much to harm it. But again, the RDA's are set for the average healthy person who doesn't ask for more than the norm from their body everyday. Athletes do!

So, are the RDA's even enough for athletes? In general, they are enough for the athlete. Not enough studies have been done to prove that any one nutrient over the RDA will help athletes perform better.[2]

Table 2
Recommended Dietary Allowances
Food and Nutrition Board, National Academy of Sciences-
*National Research Council, Revised 1989 a ***

	Males, 11-14	Males, 15-18	Males, 19-24	Females, 11-14	Females, 15-18	Females, 19-24
Ht. (in)(b)	62	69	70	62	64	65
Wt. (lb)(b)	99	145	160	101	120	128
Protein (g)	45	59	58	46	44	46
Vitamin A (mcg)(c)	1,000	1,000	1,000	800	800	800
Vitamin D (mcg)(d)	10	10	10	10	10	10
Vitamin E (mcg alpha-TE)(e)	10	10	10	8	8	8
Vitamin K (mcg)	45	65	70	45	55	60
Vitamin C (mg)	50	60	60	50	60	60
Thiamin (mg)	1.3	1.5	1.5	1.1	1.1	1.1
Riboflavin (mg)	1.5	1.8	1.7	1.3	1.3	1.3
Niacin (mg NE)(f)	17	20	19	15	15	15
Vitamin B6 (mg)	1.7	2.0	2.0	1.4	1.5	1.6
Folate (mcg)	150	200	200	150	180	180
Vitamin B12 (mcg)	2.0	2.0	2.0	2.0	2.0	2.0
Calcium (mg)	1,200	1,200	1,200	1,200	1,200	1,200
Phosphorous (mg)	1,200	1,200	1,200	1,200	1,200	1,200
Magnesium	270	400	350	280	300	280

	Males, 11-14	Males, 15-18	Males, 19-24	Females, 11-14	Females, 15-18	Females, 19-24
Iron (mg)	12	12	10	15	15	15
Zinc (mg)	15	15	15	12	12	12
Iodine (mcg)	150	150	150	150	150	150
Selenium (mcg)	40	50	70	45	50	55

a: The allowances, expressed as average daily intakes over time, are intended to provide for individual variations among most normal persons as they live in the United States under usual environmental stresses. Diets should be based on a variety of common foods in order to provide other nutrients for which human requirements have been less well defined.

b: Weights and heights of Reference Adults are actual medians for the U.S. population of the designated age, as reported by NHANES II. The median weights and heights of those under 19 years of age were taken from Hamill et al. (1979). The use of the figures does not imply that the height-to-weight ratios are ideal.

c: Retinol equivalents. 1 retinol equivalent=1mcg retinol or 6 mcg Beta-carotene.

d: As cholecalciferol. 10 mcg cholecalciferol=400IU of vitamin D.

e: Alpha tocopherol equivalents. 1 mg d-Alpha-tocopherol=1 Alpha-TE

f: 1NE (niacin equivalent) is equal to 1 mg of niacin or 60 of dietary tryptophan.

*Reprinted with permission

BREATHE A LITTLE EASIER

One nutrient that is of concern, however, is iron. Iron deficient anemia is the most common nutrient deficiency in the entire world. Forty to fifty percent of teenage female athletes show some sign of iron deficient anemia.[3] Diets that are low in red meat, beans, shellfish and dried fruits put individuals at risk for anemia. Iron's main role is to transport oxygen in the blood and throughout the body. A lack of iron can put the gymnast at a disadvantage. People who have low blood iron have been shown to tire faster during a physical task or exercise. It is important that a diet contains enough iron, but too much of a good thing is not always good. Iron can be toxic if taken in very high dosages.[3]

The nutrient chart below describes each nutrient. It gives information on where it can be found, what it does, and symptoms of not having enough of that nutrient.

Table 3

Vitamin	Best Source	Functions	Deficiency Symptoms
A (Retinol Carotene)	Liver, eggs, dark green & deep orange fruits & vegetables, dairy products	Growth & repair of body tissues (resist infection), bone & tooth formation, visual purple production (necessary for night vision)	Night blindness, drying of the eyes, dry, rough skin, impaired bone growth
B-1 (Thiamin)	Wheat germ, liver, pork, whole grains & enriched grains, dried beans	Carbohydrate metabolism, appetite maintenance, nerve function, growth & muscle tone	Mental confusion, muscle weakness, edema, fatigue, loss of appetite
B-2 (Riboflavin)	Dairy products, green leafy vegetables, whole grains & enriched grains	Necessary for fat, carbohydrate & protein metabolism, cell respiration, formation of antibodies & red blood cells	Sensitivity of eyes to light, cracks in corners of mouth, dermatitis around nose, lips
B-6 (Pyridoxine)	Fish, poultry, lean meat whole grains	Necessary for fat, carbohydrate & protein metabolism, formation of antibodies	Dermatitis, anemia, nausea, smooth tongue
B-12 (Cobalamin)	Organ meats, lean meat, fish & poultry, eggs, dairy products	Carbohydrate, fat & protein metabolism, maintains healthy nervous system, blood cell formation	Pernicious anemia, numbness & tingling in fingers & toes

Vitamin	Best Source	Functions	Deficiency Symptoms
Biotin	Egg yolks, organ meats, dark green vegetables, made by micro-organisms in intestinal tract	Carbohydrate, fat & protein metabolism, formation of fatty acids, helps utilize B vitamins	Not seen under normal circumstances; pale, dry scaly skin, depression, poor appetite
Folic Acid	Green leafy vegetables, organ meats, dried beans	Red blood cell formation, protein metabolism, growth & cell division	Anemia, diarrhea, smooth tongue, poor growth
Niacin	Meat, poultry, fish, nuts, whole grains & enriched grains, dried beans	Fat, carbohydrate & protein metabolism, health of skin, tongue & digestive system, blood circulation	General fatigue, digestive disorders, irritability, loss of appetite, skin disorders
Pantothenic Acid	Lean meats, whole grains legumes	Converts nutrients into energy, formation of some fats, vitamin utilization	Not seen under normal circumstances; vomiting, severe abdominal cramps, fatigue, tingling hands & feet
C (Ascorbic Acid)	Citrus fruits, melon, berries, vegetables	Helps heal wounds, strengthens blood vessels, collagen maintenance, resistance to infection	Bleeding gums, slow healing wounds, bruising, aching joints, nose bleeds, anemia
D (Calciferol)	Egg yolks, organ meats, fortified milk, also made in skin exposed to sunlight	Calcium & phosphorous metabolism (bone & teeth formation)	Poor bone growth, rickets, osteomalacia, muscle twitching
E (Tocopherol)	Vegetable oils & margarine, wheat germ, nuts, dark green vegetables, whole grains	Maintains cell membranes, protects vitamin A & essential fatty acids from oxidation, red blood cell formation	Not seen in humans except after prolonged impairment of fat absorption, neurologial abnormalities
K	Green leafy vegetables, fruit, cereal, dairy products	Important in formation of blood clotting agents	Tendency to hemorrhage

Mineral	Best Source	Functions	Deficiency Symptoms
Calcium	Milk & milk products	Strong bones, teeth, muscle tissue, regulates heartbeat, muscle action & nerve function	Soft brittle bones, back & leg pains, heart palpitations, tetany blood clotting
Chromium	Brewer's yeast, cheese, whole grains, meat	Glucose metabolism (energy), increases effectiveness of insulin	Atherosclerosis, glucose intolerance in diabetics

Mineral	Best Source	Functions	Deficiency Symptoms
Copper	Oysters, nuts, organ meats, dried beans	Formation of red blood cells, bone growth & health, works with vitamin C to form elastin	Anemia, bone demineralization, nervous system disturbances
Iodine	Seafood, iodized salt	Component of hormone thyroxine which controls metabolism	Goiter, obesity
Iron	Organ meats, meat, fish, poultry, dried beans, whole grains & enriched grains, green leafy vegetables	Formation of hemoglobin in blood & myoglobin in muscles, which supply oxygen to the cells	Anemia (pale skin, fatigue)
Magnesium	Nuts, green vegetables, whole grains, dried beans	Enzyme activation, nerve & muscle function, calcium and potassium balance	Nausea, muscle weakness or twitching, irritability
Manganese	Nuts, whole grains, vegetables, fruits	Enzyme activation, carbohydrate & fat production, sex hormone production, skeletal development	Abnormal bone & cartilage formation, impaired glucose tolerance
Phosphorous	Meat, poultry, fish eggs, dairy products, dried beans, whole grains	Bone development, important in protein, fat & carbohydrate utilization	Weakness, poor appetite, bone pain
Potassium	Vegetables, fruits, dried beans, milk & yogurt	Fluid balance, controls activity of heart muscle nervous system	Lethargy, weakness, poor appetite, abnormal heart rhythm
Selenium	Seafood, organ meats, lean meats, grains	Protects body tissues against oxidative damage from radiation, pollution & normal metabolic processing	Heart muscle abnormalities
Zinc	Lean meats, liver, eggs seafood, whole grains, dairy products	Involved in many enzymes regulating metabolism, important in development of reproductive system, aids in healing	Retarded growth, prolonged wound healing, loss of appetite

AICR Guide to Vitamins and Minerals. American Institute for Cancer Research, Washington, D.C. 20009. Reprinted with permission.

WATER: PURE AND SIMPLE

Water. Something that is very basic, but needed for so many things. Unfortunately, this is one nutrient that athletes need more of but usually overlook. Water serves many purposes in the body.

Table 4: Body tissues and the percentage of water they contain

Tissue	% Water
Blood	83.0
Kidneys	82.7
Heart	79.2
Lungs	79.0
Spleen	75.8
Muscle	75.6
Brain	74.8
Intestine	74.5
Skin	72.0
Liver	68.3
Skeleton	22.0
Fat	10.0

Hickson JR and Wolinsky I. Nutrition in Exercise and Sport, Boca Raton: CRC Press, 1989. Reprinted with permission.

Many gymnasts might avoid drinking water because of the way it makes them feel during practice or competition. The jostling of it in their stomach while upside down might be annoying. This is usually caused, however, by gymnasts who wait too long, get too thirsty, and then drink too much water. This can be avoided by drinking small amounts more often during training. Making sure to drink a small amount of water every 15-20 minutes will prevent dehydration, and will increase the amount of work that your muscles can do. Remember, the more dehydrated you become, the more water your muscles will lose, the less your muscles will be able to work.

Being an athlete puts many demands on your body as well as your life. Anyone can design the perfect training schedule and have the most favorable conditions for training ever imagined. The right equipment, the best coaching and the perfect schedule cannot benefit you if you don't take proper care to get enough sleep, take care of your basic needs, and of course, eat right.

References
1. Seeley RR, Stevens TD, and Tate P. *Anatomy and Physiology.* St Louis: Times-Mirror, 1989.
2. Hickson JF, Wollinsky I. *Nutrition in Exercise and Sport.* Boca Raton: CRC Press, 1989.
3. Rowland TW. "Iron Deficiency in the Young Athlete." *Pediatric Clinics of North America.* 1990;37(5):1153-1163.

Other references
Whitney EN, Hamilton EMN, Sizer FS. *Nutrition: Concepts and Controversy.* St. Paul: West Publishing, 1982.

CHAPTER 2
Building a Pyramid to Nutrition Success

One fascination that the media have with young athletes and particularly young gymnasts is the incredibly busy schedule that they keep. A typical interview might include questions like, "What is a typical day for you like?" and "Do you have any free time?" More often than not, the athlete will list everything that they do, and leave out the fact that they eat, with the exception of dinner (mostly because of its social/family activity). It would be a safe bet to say that the athlete does eat breakfast, lunch and dinner, but the fact that it is forgotten is a good indication of how much time goes into planning meals.

Nevertheless, eating becomes a forgotten part of the day. It is usually done on the run or combined with another activity such as reading, doing homework or watching TV. These types of activities can lead to forgetful eating, or eating without paying attention. This happens most often when people watch TV. One potato chip can lead to a bag by the end of a 30-minute sitcom. It also makes it difficult to analyze a diet when you cannot remember exactly what you ate and how much you ate. Eating is something many people don't put too much thought and effort into, but good nutrition takes time and effort for it to be of any benefit.

Figure 1

Diet Analysis

Name: average gymnast 15, 5 - foot, 100 lbs practicing 5 hours per day
Start date: Fri, Jun 11, 1993
End date: Fri, Jun 11, 1993

Calorie breakdown:

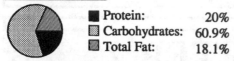

- ■ Protein: 20%
- ▨ Carbohydrates: 60.9%
- ▨ Total Fat: 18.1%

Nutrient analysis:

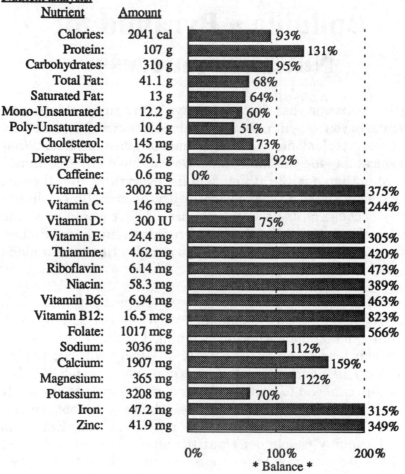

Nutrient	Amount	Balance
Calories:	2041 cal	93%
Protein:	107 g	131%
Carbohydrates:	310 g	95%
Total Fat:	41.1 g	68%
Saturated Fat:	13 g	64%
Mono-Unsaturated:	12.2 g	60%
Poly-Unsaturated:	10.4 g	51%
Cholesterol:	145 mg	73%
Dietary Fiber:	26.1 g	92%
Caffeine:	0.6 mg	0%
Vitamin A:	3002 RE	375%
Vitamin C:	146 mg	244%
Vitamin D:	300 IU	75%
Vitamin E:	24.4 mg	305%
Thiamine:	4.62 mg	420%
Riboflavin:	6.14 mg	473%
Niacin:	58.3 mg	389%
Vitamin B6:	6.94 mg	463%
Vitamin B12:	16.5 mcg	823%
Folate:	1017 mcg	566%
Sodium:	3036 mg	112%
Calcium:	1907 mg	159%
Magnesium:	365 mg	122%
Potassium:	3208 mg	70%
Iron:	47.2 mg	315%
Zinc:	41.9 mg	349%

0%   100%   200%
* Balance *

ANALYZE YOURSELF...

So what is the best way to analyze what you are eating? To analyze something is to take it apart and look at each individual piece of the whole picture. This is how a diet analysis is done. With computer technology, a diet analysis can be done quickly and the results can be read from the detailed computer printout provided by the diet analysis program. Look at Figure 1.

The biggest problem with doing a nutritional analysis is remembering what you ate so it can be analyzed correctly! If you have problems remembering exact portion sizes of food, how it was cooked, and what you even ate, an analysis won't be very accurate or helpful. It's difficult to know if your are meeting your daily needs for vitamins, minerals and calories if you cannot even remember what you had for lunch.

The best way to correctly remember what you ate during the day is to keep a 24-hour food record. This is simply a journal of the things that you eat throughout the day. The form in Figure 2 can be photocopied and used. The best way to do a food record is to make three copies of this form, and to record what you eat for three days. This can be for any three days of the week, with at least one weekend day being used. Once this is complete, it can be taken to a registered dietitian. The dietitian can then sit down with you to go over what he or she found, and how you are meeting your dietary needs. Again, this is looking at what you eat over a period of time. Looking at one day is not a good way to analyze your diet on the whole, and it is not a good average of what you really eat day to day.

Figure 2

DAILY FOOD DIARY

TIME	FOOD	AMOUNT	MEASURE	PREPARATION
Example *6:45am*	*oatmeal*	*1*	*cup*	*microwave*

What is a registered dietitian?

A registered dietitian (R.D.) is someone who has met the education standards set by the American Dietetic Association (ADA). These education standards include holding at least a Bachelor's of Science college degree in nutrition, doing an internship for a year or longer, and passing the Registered Dietitian's exam.

A "nutritionist" is a term that anyone can use. This person does not need to have any formal education to call himself a nutritionist. It is very important to look for someone who has R.D. after their name before you receive any nutrition counseling.

Once you have your diet analyzed, the job turns to finding your balance. Are you getting too much of one nutrient and not enough of the others? This is something that the R.D. can go over with you.

You can call the American Dietetic Association and they can refer you to a registered dietitian in your area. Make sure to ask for a dietitian with experience in working with athletes. The toll free number is 1-800-366-1655.

THE BALANCING ACT...

Balance is something that is very important to the gymnast, not only on the balance beam or pommel horse, but the balance that you need with a daily schedule. An eating plan requires balance as well.

Many people love to claim that they eat good foods 100% of the time, and that they wouldn't be caught dead eating foods that are high in fat and calories. However, we are all human, and we sometimes like to eat foods that are not always the smartest food choice. Balance of your eating lifestyle means making good food choices that will benefit you, and making those choices that you feel are right.

Foods also tend to pick up labels and take on personality traits from the people who eat them. Some foods have picked up labels such as "bad" and "sinful." Once somebody eats one of these foods, they tend to label themselves as "bad" or "sinful." Enjoying your birthday with a piece of birthday cake is not "being bad," and it won't jeopardize your eating plan as an athlete. It's the feeling that you can't have a piece of cake on your birthday that is not healthy. Any way you look at it, food provides us with calories, which gives us energy. This is not bad, but many of the food choices that we make are better than others. It is true that broccoli is a better food choice than a Twinkie™, and the choice to eat broccoli should be made more often than the choice to eat a Twinkie™. Making smart food choices is the key to a healthy eating plan and lifestyle.

BEING DENSE IS GOOD...

In chapter 1, we spoke of the efficiency of energy found in complex carbohydrates, and how you can get the most efficient energy from what you eat. We can also use the term efficient to describe what is called nutrient density. Nutrient density is described as an item of food that gives you many different vitamins and minerals for the calories it has. We can use the broccoli and the Twinkie™ example and say that broccoli is more nutrient dense than the Twinkie™. The broccoli is low in calories, but has more vitamins and minerals to offer. Another example is the fast-food hamburger. A fast-food hamburger may give you all of the protein that you need for the entire day, but it also gives you a high amount of fat. This is not efficient, and it is not as nutrient dense as a lean piece of meat. Refer to Figure 3 for the calorie analysis of a Twinkie and broccoli.

The best way to chose those foods that are nutrient dense is to look at the list provided in Table 3 from Chapter 1. This lists the foods that contain those vitamins and minerals that we need, and the best foods to get them from.

Figure 3

Diet Analysis
1 Twinkie ™
143 calories

Calorie breakdown:

■ Protein:	3.45%
▨ Carbohydrates:	70.4%
▧ Total Fat:	26.1%

Nutrient analysis:

Nutrient	Amount	
Calories:	143 cal	9%
Protein:	1.25 g	2%
Carbohydrates:	25.5 g	10%
Total Fat:	4.2 g	9%
Saturated Fat:	1.65 g	11%
Mono-Unsaturated:	1.75 g	11%
Poly-Unsaturated:	0.42 g	3%
Cholesterol:	21 mg	12%
Dietary Fiber:	0.3 g	1%
Caffeine:	0 mg	0%
Vitamin A:	4.05RE	1%
Vitamin C:	0.6 mg	1%
Vitamin D:	0 IU	0%
Vitamin E:	0 mg	0%
Thiamine:	0.06 mg	5%
Riboflavin:	0.068 mg	5%
Niacin:	0.5 mg	3%
Vitamin B6:	0 mg	0%
Vitamin B12:	0.2 mcg	10%
Folate:	8 mcg	4%
Sodium:	189 mg	7%
Calcium:	19 mg	2%
Magnesium:	3.55 mg	1%
Potassium:	60 mg	1%
Iron:	0.55 mg	4%
Zinc:	0.25 mg	2%

0%   100%   200%
* Balance *

Diet Analysis
3 cups of Broccoli
138 calories

<u>Calorie breakdown:</u>

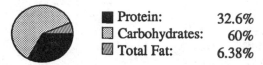

■ Protein:	32.6%
▨ Carbohydrates:	60%
▧ Total Fat:	6.38%

<u>Nutrient analysis:</u>

<u>Nutrient</u>   <u>Amount</u>

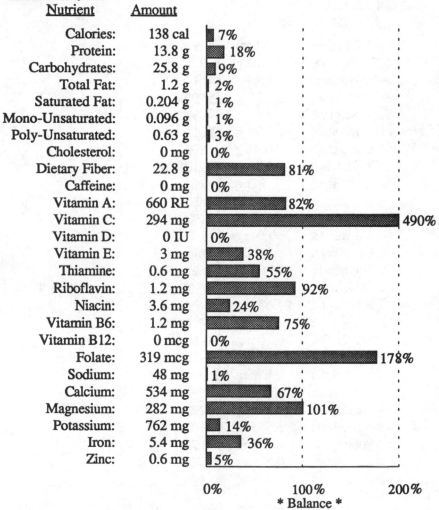

Nutrient	Amount	Balance
Calories:	138 cal	7%
Protein:	13.8 g	18%
Carbohydrates:	25.8 g	9%
Total Fat:	1.2 g	2%
Saturated Fat:	0.204 g	1%
Mono-Unsaturated:	0.096 g	1%
Poly-Unsaturated:	0.63 g	3%
Cholesterol:	0 mg	0%
Dietary Fiber:	22.8 g	81%
Caffeine:	0 mg	0%
Vitamin A:	660 RE	82%
Vitamin C:	294 mg	490%
Vitamin D:	0 IU	0%
Vitamin E:	3 mg	38%
Thiamine:	0.6 mg	55%
Riboflavin:	1.2 mg	92%
Niacin:	3.6 mg	24%
Vitamin B6:	1.2 mg	75%
Vitamin B12:	0 mcg	0%
Folate:	319 mcg	178%
Sodium:	48 mg	1%
Calcium:	534 mg	67%
Magnesium:	282 mg	101%
Potassium:	762 mg	14%
Iron:	5.4 mg	36%
Zinc:	0.6 mg	5%

0%　　　　100%　　　　200%
* Balance *

FOOD GUIDE PYRAMID...

Recently, the Department of Health and Human Services introduced a guide for eating that replaces the Basic Four food groups. It is called the Food Guide Pyramid, and it is designed to show the importance of fruits, vegetables and grains by placing them at the base of the pyramid, which represents the base of our diet. The pyramid suggests that we eat 6-11 servings of breads and cereals each day. The base is also supported by generous servings of fruits (2-4), and vegetables (3-5). As we near the top of the pyramid, the boxes become smaller, meaning that we need less meat servings (2-3), milk/milk product servings (2-3), and least of all, fats, oils, and sweets (to be used occasionally). See Figure 4, the Food Guide Pyramid

Researchers have learned the importance of complex carbohydrates, and that Americans eat much more protein and fat than needed. Therefore, the new pyramid has been made to show these new findings.

These recommendations may seem like a lot of food to eat, but also take note of the serving sizes. By having a bowl of cereal and two pieces of toast for breakfast, you have already reached three to four servings of grains for the day.

Figure 5 lists the pyramid suggested servings according to the calories that you eat. It also lists a higher carbohydrate eating plan that is closer to meeting the 62-65% carbohydrate, 15-18% protein, and 20% or less fat recommendation for athletes.

CALORIE NEEDS...

Because the RDA's do not include recommendations for energy, we must calculate these using your height, weight, age, and activity level. Here is a quick reference to calculate how many calories you need each day. You will probably need a calculator:

For girls:
655 + (4.36 x your weight in pounds) + (4.7 x your height in inches) - 4.7 x your age

Figure 4

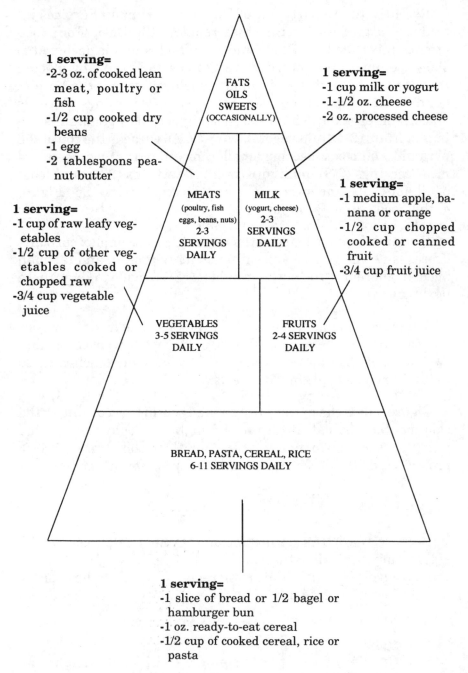

1 serving=
-2-3 oz. of cooked lean meat, poultry or fish
-1/2 cup cooked dry beans
-1 egg
-2 tablespoons peanut butter

1 serving=
-1 cup milk or yogurt
-1-1/2 oz. cheese
-2 oz. processed cheese

1 serving=
-1 cup of raw leafy vegetables
-1/2 cup of other vegetables cooked or chopped raw
-3/4 cup vegetable juice

1 serving=
-1 medium apple, banana or orange
-1/2 cup chopped cooked or canned fruit
-3/4 cup fruit juice

FATS
OILS
SWEETS
(OCCASIONALLY)

MEATS
(poultry, fish eggs, beans, nuts)
2-3
SERVINGS
DAILY

MILK
(yogurt, cheese)
2-3
SERVINGS
DAILY

VEGETABLES
3-5 SERVINGS
DAILY

FRUITS
2-4 SERVINGS
DAILY

BREAD, PASTA, CEREAL, RICE
6-11 SERVINGS DAILY

1 serving=
-1 slice of bread or 1/2 bagel or hamburger bun
-1 oz. ready-to-eat cereal
-1/2 cup of cooked cereal, rice or pasta

For example, a female gymnast who is 15 years old, is 5'0" and who weighs 100 lbs...

655 + (4.36 x 100) + (4.7 x 60) - (4.7 x 15) =
655 + 436 + 282 - 70.5 = 1302.5 calories

Then you must add 2.5 calories for every minute that you practice. So, if you practice for 5 hours each day, your calorie needs are:

5 hours x 60 minutes per hour = 300 minutes of practice
300 x 2.5 calories per minute = 750 calories
1302.5 calories + 750 calories = 2052.5 calories needed per day.

For boys
66.0 + (6.23 x your weight in pounds) + (12.7 x your height in
     inches) - 6.8 x your age

Then add 2.8 calories for every minute that you practice For example, a male gymnast who is 18 years old, who is 5'5" and who weighs 138 lbs and who practices for 5 hours...

 66.0 + (6.23 x 138) + (12.7 x 65) - (6.8 x 18) =
66.0 + 859 + 826 - 122.4 = 1628.6 calories
5 hours x 60 minutes per hour = 300 minutes
300 x 2.8 calories per minute = 840 calories
1628.6 calories + 840 calories = 2468.6 calories

You might want to sit down with your coach to figure this out so you can both get a good idea of how many calories you need to eat each day.

Source: Dr. Dan Benardot, Ph.D., RD, LD. Georgia State University

BUT HOW DO I FIND THE TIME?

It is one thing to have information to use on nutrition. To be able to use this information is a completely different subject. It would be wonderful to have the time to plan meals and to take more than 30 minutes to eat. But is this reality? Probably not for most gymnasts.

Figure 5

SAMPLE DIETS

These are sample diets of what the Pyramid suggests, and a higher carbohydrate version that is more closely in line with the **62-65%** carbohydrate, **15-18%** protein, and **20% or <** fat goal for athletes.

	1600 calorie pyramid suggestion (number of servings)	1600 calorie high carbohydrate (number of servings)
Bread	6	9
Vegetables	3	4
Fruits	2	4
Milk	2-3	2(nonfat)
Meats (oz)	5	3
Fat (total) (grams)	53	41
Fat (extra)(grams)	---	26

	2200 calorie pyramid suggestion (number of servings)	2200 calorie high carbohydrate (number of servings)
Bread	9	13
Vegetables	4	5
Fruits	3	6
Milk	2-3	3 (nonfat)
Meat (oz)	6	4
Fat (total)(grams)	73	56
Fat (extra)(grams)	---	36

	2800 calorie pyramid suggestion (number of servings)	2800 calorie high carbohydrate (number of servings)
Bread	11	15
Vegetables	5	6
Fruits	4	8
Milk	2-3	3(nonfat)
Meat (oz)	7	5
Fat (total)(grams)	93	72
Fat (extra)(grams)	---	47

This is where strategic planning comes in to play. The planning of what to eat and when to eat may take some time, but it will benefit you in the long run. To prevent glycogen levels from getting too low, eating more than three times a day will help keep them at the level that you need for training. This may mean 5-6 small meals throughout the day, and more planning of what you eat, but the benefit will be increased energy levels.

SO YOUR MOTHER TOLD YOU NOT TO SNACK....

Snacking may be thought of as a "bad habit." Again, snacking provides calories, which is not bad. It is what is chosen for a snack that can turn snacking into a good habit or bad habit. Snacking in this case can be a great way to get the calories that you need, and to keep your energy level up. Snacks that can be chosen that are quick, easy and take only a few minutes to get ready include:

-crackers (low fat)	-fruit (any type)
-dry cereal	-bagels
-pretzels	-air popped popcorn
-raw vegetables	-dried fruit

These are just a few suggestions, but they are probably the most sensible because they travel well, they are easy to fix, they are good sources of carbohydrates and they are low in fat.

Finding time to snack may also be a problem. With a busy schedule of practice and school, snacking can be helpful if you find the time. Quick time frames can include:

-after morning practice	-in between classes at school
-halfway through practice*	-before afternoon practice
-on your ride to the gym	-before bed

*You may think, "I can't have a snack during practice, what will my coach say?" Hopefully, you and your coach are learning from this book together, and he or she will agree that snacking during practice is something that you should take time to do! Plan a time, about halfway through practice, where you can take a snack break. Also, snacking before bed if you are hungry will help you to replace glycogen levels as well.

Remember, balance includes pulling in many different pieces of your life to find a lifestyle and schedule that satisfies you. Balance in your diet is the same. The snacks that you choose, the time and effort that you take to plan your meals and the balance of your diet are decisions that you must make for yourself and for the success you decide you want.

CHAPTER 3
Road Trip Nutrition

During competition season, gymnasts may find themselves doing a lot of traveling. Whether it be a two hour car drive or a two day plane trip, it still means changes in your entire schedule. Sleeping in a different bed, eating different food and being in a different environment all together takes some adjustment. You can make this adjustment easier for yourself, especially with the foods that you choose to eat.

Eating habits often change when people travel, and they usually don't change for the better. This different schedule may cause you to eat at different times and in many different places. You will also have a wider variety of foods to choose from. This can definitely work to your advantage, if you make wise choices. However, poor food selections may lead to high fat, high calorie meals, and snacks which could ultimately affect your performance.

Eating away from home can have its advantages and its disadvantages. Here are just a few:

ADVANTAGES	DISADVANTAGES
1. There is a wider variety of dishes	1. These foods are not as familiar
2. You get to try new dishes	2. Dishes are usually higher in fat and calories
3. You don't have to prepare food	3. You have less control of what goes into the dish
4. You can ask for a dish to be prepared the way you want	4. The restaurant may not have what you want to eat
5. There is less hassle in fixing meals	5. It is harder to find good snacks when you're traveling

RESTAURANT WISDOM

While there are advantages and disadvantages to eating out, planning what you choose to eat can make dining out a big plus. Asking questions about certain dishes and making special requests should be a routine part of ordering in a restaurant. Remember, when you are in a restaurant you are paying not only for the food but the service of the food as well. Restaurants can usually fill your requests (with a few limits) and they should be happy to do so.

Here are some choices that you can make in a restaurant to lower the fat and increase the carbohydrates in your meal:

APPETIZERS
-Ask for bread or rolls as an appetizer.
-Don't be fooled by the vegetable appetizers (such as fried zucchini and onion rings) as well as cheese-filled appetizers. They are filled with fat and the vegetables may barely equal one serving.
-Skip the appetizer altogether, or order soup or a dinner salad as your appetizer.

SOUPS
-Avoid cream-based soups. Anything that says "cream of" or any of the white chowders usually use whole milk, butter and cream, and they are high in fat and calories.
-Stick with the clear broth soups and soups that include beans. Some good choices include black bean, lentil, gazpacho (cold Spanish soup), and vegetable.

SALADS
-Ask for your salad dressing on the side. This way you can control how much dressing you use.
-Be careful about ordering salads that contain high amounts of cheese and meat. The amount of fat found in these salads tends to be very high. These are salads such as Chef, Taco and Cobb.
-Choose salads that are filled with fresh vegetables such as a garden salad, or a salad that contains lean meat such as a Grilled Chicken salad.

-Ask for bread with your salad to increase your carbohydrates.

-Ask for their choices of low fat/low calorie dressings. Remember that white dressings are usually mayonnaise-based and higher in fat.

-If you choose to build your own salad at the salad bar, load up on fresh fruits and vegetables and be careful not to make it into a fat festival with high-calorie cheeses, pre-made salads (such as potato and macaroni), and high-fat salad dressings.

SANDWICHES

-Ask for condiments (such as mayonnaise, mustard, ketchup) on the side.

-Choose a lower fat cheese such as part skim mozzarella (see table 1) or go cheese-less.

-Don't choose grilled sandwiches. They tend to be higher in fat because they contain high-fat cheeses (for better melting) and butter (for grilling).

-Ask for whole grain or whole wheat bread. It is higher in fiber and contains its original vitamins and minerals.

MAIN ENTREES

-Ask for sauces on the side if they are not already part of the dish.

-When ordering a dish, make sure that you ask about the preparation styles:

-Stay away from foods that are:

-Fried	-Breaded
-Sautéed	-Buttered

-Choose those foods that are:

-Baked	-Broiled
-Poached	-Boiled
-Steamed	-Braised in broth

-Order items a la carte rather than ordering them as main entrees.

DESSERTS

-Pick those desserts that tend to be lower in fat such as:

-Sorbets	-Fruit ices
-Angel food cake	-Fresh Fruit
-Sherbets	

-Again, don't be fooled by the "vegetable desserts" such as carrot cake and zucchini bread. They are made with the same oil and fat as regular cakes and baked goods, and the amount of carrot or zucchini in the dessert is not enough to make up a serving of vegetables.

-If a certain high-calorie dessert really catches your eye, ask for extra spoons and share it with friends.

SPECIFIC RESTAURANTS:

Italian:
-Choose your pastas with tomato/marinara sauce.

-Again beware of the color white. White sauces such as Alfredo are made with cream and butter and are high in fat.

-Skip on the dishes that include high-fat meats and sausages. These dishes may include titles like prosciutto, pancetta and carbonara.

Chinese:
-Order dishes made mainly with vegetables.

-Avoid items that are breaded and/or deep fried such as sweet and sour dishes, egg rolls, and Chow Mein

-Order plain white rice instead of fried rice.

Mexican:
-Go easy on the chips before the meal, or just say "no thank you."

-Ask the restaurant if they offer beans without fat, like black beans or pinto beans in water. If they do, ask if they can substitute them into your dish in place of refried beans (which in most cases are made with lard and are high in fat).

-Ask for corn tortillas instead of flour tortillas for your dish. They are lower in fat because they are not made with lard.

SNACKING ON THE ROAD

Snacking, as you found out earlier, is very important for replacing the carbohydrate you use during exercise. Snacking and meals are usually interrupted when you travel. You can keep snacks available to you by packing them for the road, and it just

Table 1: Cheese do's and don'ts Cheese is a good source of calcium, but it is also high in fat. Out of a list of 38 cheeses, here are the top five and the bottom five cheeses according to the amount of calcium they have for each gram of fat. The score is just a way to compare the different cheeses to each other. A high score means you are getting more calcium for the amount of fat the cheese contains, and a low score means less calcium for the amount of fat the cheese contains.

Your best bets. These cheeses have the highest amount of calcium for each gram of fat that they contain. Not all of these cheeses are low fat, but they have the best scores when it comes to looking at the amount of calcium they have for each gram of fat.

Cheese	Fat (g) per 100 calories	Ca (mg) per 100 calories	Score
Cottage, 1% fat	1.4	84.1	60.1
Parmesan, hard	6.6	302.7	45.9
Mozzarella, part skim	6.3	254.2	40.3
Romano	6.9	274.5	39.8
Swiss	7.3	254.2	34.8

Maybe not. These cheeses have a much lower amount of calcium per gram of fat than the ones above. These are not your best choices when it comes to choosing a cheese as a source of calcium.

Cheese	Fat (g) per 100 calories	Ca (mg) per 100 calories	Score
Gjetost	6.4	85.6	13.4
Cream, light	7.6	61.3	8.1
Brie	8.3	54.7	6.6
Neufchatel	8.9	28.4	3.2
Cream	10.0	23.0	2.3

Adapted from Bowes & Church's Food Values of Portions Commonly Used, 15th ed. by Jean Pennington, 1989, Philadelphia, PA: J.B. Lippincott Co. with permission from the publisher.

takes a little planning. Unfortunately, not all snack foods are suited for traveling. Some tips on choosing snack items to pack include:

-Items that are high in carbohydrate (60-65%) and low in fat (20-25%).
-Items that are nonperishable (that do not spoil).
-Items that do not need refrigeration.
-Items that are easy to pack into a plastic bag, or prepackaged items.
-Foods that are familiar to you.

Some of those foods that make great snacks like this include:

-Bagels.
-Low-fat crackers. Remember, no more than 2.0-2.5 grams of fat per 100 calories.
-Fresh Fruits. Apples, bananas, oranges, tangerines, apricots, and pears are just some of the fruits that are great to pack, along with seasonal fruits such as grapes, peaches, plums, and nectarines. However, fresh fruits should be eaten within the first three days of the trip.
-Prepackaged, individual servings of fruit cocktail or applesauce.
-Individually canned fruit juices.
-Pretzels, thin or Bavarian style.
-Fat-free granola or granola bars — some of the major cereal companies are making low fat and fat free granolas that are very tasty.
-Low sugar cereals — (cereals without sugar coating) in individual boxes.

Snacks such as these can be easily packed. Obviously, it takes more planning to travel by airplane. If you are traveling by car, the possibilities are endless with the use of a cooler. This can increase your list of snacks to include yogurt, cottage cheese, and fruits that need some preparation (such as pineapple, cantaloupe, and other melons). Make sure that you choose foods that you are familiar with before a practice or competition. Popcorn and dried fruits can be great snacks but sometimes can be difficult to digest, and it may not be a wise choice before practice or competition.

INTERNATIONAL TRAVEL AND CUISINE

If you are fortunate enough to travel outside of the country, there are some important things you might want to remember. You will be introduced to a different culture that includes foods that may be unfamiliar to you.

First, ask if the tap water is drinkable. Your coach or delegation leader should know this, so ask them about the types of water you can drink. In terms of foods, one food that you may find different is the milk. Some countries use goat's milk. If you are very picky about your milk you may want to bring along nonfat dried milk, which you can find in your grocery store in individual packets. As far as snacks go, you can pack the ones listed on the previous page. However, you may want to leave fruits at home due to customs regulations in various countries.

In most European countries one of the foods that can be found at breakfast, lunch and dinner is bread. Eat up! Asian countries have rice as their staple (or main) food, which is also a great carbohydrate food. The most important thing to remember while traveling internationally is to enjoy your trip and to take a taste of the different foods that are considered specialties of that country!

Water is also very important in this picture as well. Sports bottles are very popular and easy to find as well as easy to pack. It is a convenient way to make sure that you always have water available to you.

Snack planning also means that you must be a smart shopper. This means reading food labels as you choose your snacks. Take a trip to the grocery store with your mom or dad, pick up boxes and packages of some of your favorite snacks and read the labels. You will be surprised to see what the packages may claim. Then compare these claims to what you really find on the nutrition label. The word "light" or "lite" can mean anything from light in calories to light in color. Read the label for yourself to see what you're really getting from the food. In 1994, terms like "light" and "low-fat" came to be used under strict guidelines from the Food and Drug Administration and almost all foods are required to have nutrition labels.

ERGOGENIC SNACKS

Ergogenic means "energy producing," and many companies who make ergogenic snacks have become very popular in the last two to three years. Companies such as PowerBar and Exceed have developed ergogenic snack bars that athletes can eat before, during and after a practice or competition. They are high in carbohydrates, low in fat, and they are meant for replacing glycogen stores lost during heavy exercise. This is certainly something that can be included as a snack for gymnasts, even though it's mainly targeted at endurance athletes such as marathoners and triathletes. If you decide to include these types of snacks into your eating plan, here are some tips to remember:

-Eat normal meals and use these as a snack, not a meal replacement.

-Follow the directions on the package. Many of these snack bars suggest that you drink water after eating the bar. This is important because the water helps the bar to digest properly.

-Look at the cost. Some of these bars are very expensive when you compare them to eating a piece of fruit or some crackers.

VENDING MACHINES

Vending machines can be a lifesaver for hunger in some instances, but behind that shiny machine lurks a high-fat trap. Dining by pushing buttons is not very appetizing, and it can leave you feeling unsatisfied while giving you mainly fat calories. Hopefully, through smart snacking, this hunger attack can be avoided. Figure 1 lists different types of foods that can be found in a vending machine and their fat content. Compare this to the amount

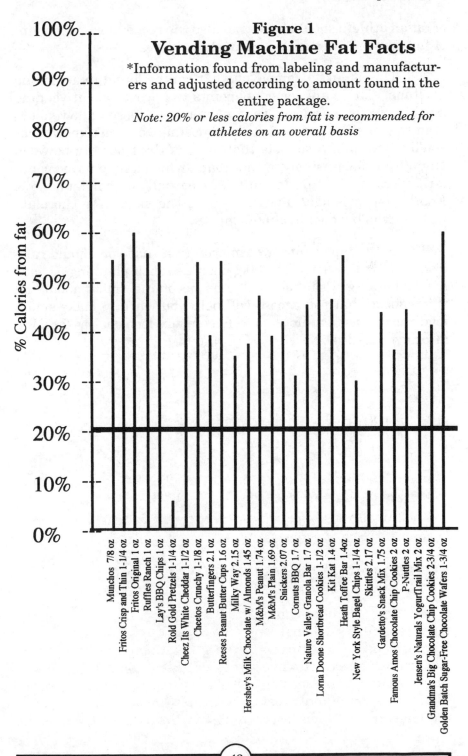

Figure 1
Vending Machine Fat Facts
*Information found from labeling and manufacturers and adjusted according to amount found in the entire package.
Note: 20% or less calories from fat is recommended for athletes on an overall basis

of fat an athlete should have, and also the recommended amount of fat that the average American should have.

This is just a sample of what can be found in a vending machine. There are some key points to uncover about vending machine foods. Because a vending machine doesn't allow you to read the labels of the food you're choosing, you don't know what you'll be getting. Also, note that most of the foods are between 45-60% fat. Surprisingly, granola bars, which have enjoyed popularity because they are "natural," are actually high in fat at 45%. Another surprisingly high-fat item is the sugar-free chocolate wafers, which weigh in at 60% fat.

The most important bit of information that you should take from here is that snacking takes just as much planning as your meal planning. Reading labels and becoming smart about the snack foods that you choose will help you learn to make smart food choices as an athlete, as well as future food choices for a life after gymnastics.

CHAPTER 4
How To Win While Losing

This chapter is a good chapter to share with your coaches. In it you will find information about healthy weight maintenance and nutrition, as well detecting signs of eating disorders. By sharing this with your coach, you can both work to create healthy eating attitudes while maintaining a good competitive weight.

Compare gymnasts from the late 1960s to gymnasts today. Ludmilla Tourischeva and Vera Caslasvka were champions in their day, but they were also women in their 20s and 30s who had more mature body types.

This accepted image was forever altered when, at the 1972 Olympic Games, the world fell in love with a little girl named Olga Korbut. She didn't win the competition, but she won many hearts with her girlish body-type and innocent style. In 1976, Nadia Comaneci showed that a 14-year-old could handle the pressures of Olympic competition, receiving seven scores of perfect 10.00, and eventually winning three Olympic gold medals.

Every year, athletes outperform their previous competition in difficulty and precision. To keep up with the innovations in gymnastics, officials update the scoring rules after each Olympic Games and the equipment is constantly improved. Today, the technical requirements of the sport have evolved to attract the athlete with the small and lean body type.

The pressure to keep weight low while increasing strength and speed may put gymnasts in the position of reaching a body weight below normal levels. Since most female gymnasts are under 20 years of age, they will experience normal growth spurts throughout their gymnastics experience. Our bodies are genetically programmed to be a certain size and shape. Some gymnasts will experience more growth than others.

Healthy weight maintenance can be beneficial for a gymnast. Weight loss beyond reasonable limits is not healthy when your body is genetically programmed to be a certain size.

Taller gymnasts can certainly have successful competitive careers. Gymnasts like Svetlana Boguinskaya, Tracee Talavera and Betty Okino became Olympic and World Championship medalists while towering over their competitors by four to five inches. During times of growth, however, it is important to maintain healthy eating habits. Proper nutrition can be one of your greatest connections to maintaining a winning attitude and achieving successful performance. Poor nutrition is a quick detour off the road to success. It can not only prevent you from reaching your athletic goals but it can contribute to severe, long term physical and emotional illnesses. Abnormal eating patterns, if left unchecked, can lead to an eating disorder.

An eating disorder is a compulsive eating pattern or habit that, when left untreated, can lead to physical and mental disease. The three most common types of eating disorders are anorexia nervosa, bulimia nervosa and bulimarexia. Eating disorders are most typically found in young females from age 12 through college age. The images found in magazines, on TV and throughout society can put pressure on young girls to be thin. Aspiring young gymnasts may feel pressure to have the perfect gymnastics body type by watching top level gymnasts on TV or by seeing pictures in gymnastics magazines. This pressure, whether internal or external, if not handled properly, may lead to one of these three disorders. Any of these disorders can begin with the very innocent goal of wanting to lose a few pounds.

Anorexia nervosa is a condition where a person starves themselves, and they purposely ignore hunger in the quest to lose weight. People who suffer from anorexia are most often very intelligent overachievers with an intense desire to succeed. Young girls and boys who receive these positive comments for their discipline to maintain a low weight may take the weight loss too far. This results in a dramatic weight loss, sometimes more than one fourth of their original body weight.[1] As the weight loss continues, the young person changes their physical and emotional outlook. Weight loss becomes another achievable goal with no end in sight. The harder a person works toward this weight loss, the more challenging the weight loss becomes. Without established goals and guidelines from a knowledgeable source, an unhealthy cycle can develop (See Figure 1).

Figure 1: Cycle of an eating disorder

 Desire to lose weight

Attention from weight loss   Decreased food intake

          Weight loss

As you can tell, the cycle leads to weight loss down to dangerously low levels. In the healthy stages of weight control, gymnastics may become easier. For an anorexic, however, continued weight loss will include a decrease of both fat and muscle. A number of other side effects that are extremely dangerous to health will also occur (See Table 1). Anorexia nervosa is a condition that can only be treated by seeking professional help.

Table 1: Effects of eating disorders on athletic performance:

-Glycogen depletion: Constant starvation of muscle tissues will result in lowered glycogen stores. This ultimately results in depleted energy that is never replaced because carbohydrates are not eaten.

-Metabolic abnormalities: Starving oneself results in the body's need for energy from muscle tissue. This includes all muscles in the body, including the heart. Electrolyte imbalance can also result in heart irregularities. Sudden death can be a result of these metabolic changes.

-Decrease in lean body mass: If an athlete becomes anorexic and undereats calories, the body must use lean body mass for energy (protein from the muscles). If any weight is regained, which might happen in bulimics who stop purging, this weight is regained mostly as fat. A constant cycling effect takes place, and lean body mass is continually lost while fat is continually gained.

From *Coaches Guide to Nutrition and Weight Control*, 2nd Ed. (pp. 116-117) by P.A. Eisenman, S.C. Johnson, and J.E. Benson, Champaign, IL: Leisure Press. Copyright 1990 by Patricia A. Eisenman, Stephen C. Johnson, and Joan E. Benson. Adapted and reprinted by permission of Human Kinetics Publishers.

Bulimia is another type of eating disorder where a person eats very large quantities of food (bingeing) followed by purging (getting rid of it) by using laxatives, vomiting or intense exercise. Unlike anorexia, bulimia is not as easy to detect. Most bulimics are of normal body weight. Their activity of bingeing and purging can lead to very extreme consequences, such as those described in Table 1. Bingeing and purging behaviors become very addictive, and it, too, can only be treated by seeking professional help.

The third component, bulimarexia or anorexia with the bulimia subtype, is a combination of self-starvation and the use of purging techniques as well as intense exercise to induce weight loss. Bulimarexia is the most dangerous of the three because of the combination of undereating and purging activity.[2] The form of bulimarexia associated with intense exercise is also known as anorexia athletic, because of the tendency of athletic individuals to use this as a form of weight control.[3]

Because gymnasts are in a sport that focuses on body size and body image, they are often placed in a "risk" category for eating disorders. This is also true for sports like dancing, swimming, figure skating, diving, and distance running.

TO THE GYMNAST ABOUT EATING DISORDERS

It is important to understand the harmful effects of eating disorders. They are physically damaging as well as emotionally traumatic. An eating disorder can take over your life and create damaging consequences. Be aware of the signs and beliefs that put you at risk for an eating disorder:

-**Constant worry about what you eat:** It is important to be very thoughtful of the food choices you make. Planning meals takes time, but thinking about food all day long can be a distraction to your daily schedule. On your days off, try eating when you're hungry rather than eating by a schedule, keeping in mind to eat high-carbohydrate, low-fat foods for your next day of training.

-**Constant worry about what the scale says:** Weight can easily shift between 2 to 3 pounds each day due to water weight. Constantly checking your weight on the scale can lead to unnecessary worry about how much you weigh. Checking your weight once a week is a more reliable way to detect fat gain or loss.

-**Worrying about what others think of your body:** Many people are concerned about their physical appearance and how they look to others. This is something that many non-athletes think about on a regular basis. If this is your main reason for wanting to lose weight, you might want to ask yourself why you feel this way. As a gymnast, being both physically and mentally comfortable with yourself is a key to your success in this sport. Feel good about your body for yourself and not for anyone else. Feeling confident with yourself for you and not anyone else will make you the best athlete you can possibly be.

-**Attaching your scale weight to your self worth:** Attaching feelings of guilt or shame to what you eat is a defeating process. Don't let the scale determine your self worth! Your eating habits should not determine how you feel about yourself. Food provides us with nourishment, and we eat to help support good health. Remember, we eat to live, not live to eat.

-**Don't feel ashamed for growing:** As you get older, your body will grow. Because gymnastics is such a big part of your life right now, the growth may be a difficult challenge for you. This is very normal and it happens to everyone. Trying to control this growth by restricting your eating will lead to worse consequences than the growth itself. Allow your body to find its genetic potential, and feed your body what it needs.

Eating disorders not only cause problems in the present, but they can also have serious consequences for your future. Having an eating disorder may effect your brain health, bone health, and your ability to have children. The years that you spend doing gymnastics make up a very small portion of your life. You are a person with many dimensions and gifts, and you have a lifetime to develop them. The picture of your life is much bigger than just your gymnastics career. Having an eating disorder is not worth jeopardizing your future goals and desires!

TO THE COACHES ABOUT EATING DISORDERS

It is important for you as a coach to understand that your athletes look to you for guidance not only for gymnastics but for behavior as well. Although you may not possess the skills of a nutrition expert, inform yourself about the nutrition status of your athletes. Take action in situations that may be putting your athletes at a physical or psychological risk by finding a nutritional expert to help your athletes.

-**Your influence on athletes is tremendous.** Consider carefully the comments you make to your athletes about weight issues. Your athletes may take these comments personally, which could lead them to an abnormal eating behavior. Gymnasts value their coach's opinion and advice. A negative or teasing word about weight can be devastating. Many athletes with eating disorders can remember a specific comment made by a coach that triggered their adverse eating behavior. Even subtle references can be taken the wrong way. Be aware of all issues that affect your gymnast when handling situations that deal with body weight. Remember, you are a teacher and every move you make in your classroom sets an example.

-**Be accountable.** If you suspect your athlete is suffering from an eating disorder, don't wait to see if it goes away. If not given professional attention, eating disorders progressively worsen. You should not try to handle it yourself. See Table 2 for tips on how to detect an eating disorder. Find a qualified professional to make an official diagnosis and insist that your athlete gets counseling if he or she does indeed have an eating disorder.

-**Punishment may spur adverse behavior.** Punishment for being over competitive weight may result in the athlete developing an unhealthy relationship with food. It can mean the difference between eating well to lose weight and not eating enough to maintain health. Give the gymnast positive encouragement to eat the right foods so that she or he can maintain health while reaching their competitive weight.

-**Give your athletes the best.** If your gymnast is over or under competitive weight or needs specialized nutrition information, provide professional resources such as the individual attention of a registered dietitian. If you demand the best from your athletes in terms of performance, then make sure you are giving them the best in terms of professional knowledge for optimum training.

-**Be sensitive to the growing athlete.** It is hard for the gymnast experiencing a growth spurt to accept that gymnastics is becoming more difficult. In one research study, gymnasts who had outgrown their gymnastics peers suffered additional emotional stress because they no longer fit into the comfortable, well-known mold of a gymnast.[4] Added pressure from a coach can make it worse. Be supportive of that athlete and look for opportunities at which the gymnast can excel during these growing years.

-Separate the gymnast's challenge with weight from other aspects of achieving success in the gym. The gymnast who may have trouble achieving the ideal competitive weight needs to have positive experiences from which she or he can draw motivation. Constant punishment in other areas of training is an uncomfortable reminder of the weight issue and it could lead to an unhealthy focus on losing weight.

Table 2

Warning signs for Anorexia Nervosa:

Behavioral *
-A preoccupation with food, calories, and weight
-Wearing baggy or layered clothing
-Relentless, excessive exercise
-Mood swings
-Avoiding food-related social activities

Physical **
-Weight loss of unknown origin
-Stopping of menstrual period
-Low metabolism, tendency to always be cold
-Changes in skin, thinning of hair on face, arms
-Constipation
-Disruptive sleep

Warning signs for Bulimia Nervosa:

Behavioral *
-Excessive concern about weight
-Bathroom visits after meals
-Depressive moods
-Strict dieting followed by eating binges
-Increasing criticism of one's body

Physical **
-Normal body size
-Poor athletic performance
-Dehydration, electrolyte imbalance
-Throat/dental problems
-Swollen glands/chipmunk appearance

The presence of one or two of these signs does not necessarily indicate the presence of an eating disorder. Absolute diagnosis should be done by appropriate professionals

*Source: National Collegiate Athletic Association, Overland Park, KS, 1992.

** Note. *From Coaches Guide to Nutrition and Weight Control*, 2nd Ed. (pp. 112-115) by P.A. Eisenman, S.C. Johnson, and J.E. Benson, Champaign, IL: Leisure Press. Copyright 1990 by Patricia A. Eisenman, Stephen C. Johnson, and Joan E. Benson. Adapted and reprinted by permission of Human Kinetics Publishers.

HOW TO ACHIEVE IDEAL COMPETITIVE WEIGHT...SAFELY

Do you feel you are not at your competitive weight? Do you know what a good competitive weight is for yourself? The best place to start is by asking yourself, "At what weight do I feel strong, and able to perform all of my skills?" It is important to focus first on a weight that feels good. Occasionally use the numbers on the scale as a reference for ideal weight. You can also find that ideal competitive body weight through the help of a registered dietitian who is experienced with athletes.

Ideal body weight is very individualized. Because two people are the same height does not mean they should have the same ideal body weight. Determine your ideal body weight according to what works best for you.

If you do come to the conclusion that you are not at your optimum competitive weight goal, set a reasonable time frame in which to reach that goal. You should not attempt to lose or gain more than one pound per week. Your ideal weight may change as weight loss occurs. Make sure to be flexible with your goals, and to be in tune with the way you feel, not with the numbers on the scale.

To achieve weight loss, one or two things must happen. One must decrease the amount of calories eaten, and/or increase the amount of calories burned. Both of these can be done in combination to see the best result. To gain weight, the opposite would have to take place (increasing calories and decreasing the amount of calories burned).

Weight Loss

Because gymnasts are young and need to meet their daily nutrient requirements, a big decrease in calories is not the smartest way to lose weight. A slight decrease in calories (by no more than 200), along with a slight increase in an aerobic-type exercise (such as a brisk walk or moderate bike ride for 30-45 minutes) could be the best combination for healthy weight loss. You should NEVER eat less than 1200 calories if you're a female and 1500 for a male.

Weight Gain

For weight gain, one should increase the amount of calories eaten by choosing foods that are good sources of carbohydrates. If you still find that you need to increase the calories for more weight gain, adding fat to your foods may help. Eating peanut butter and choosing whole dairy products such as whole milk are two ways of doing this.

To find out how many calories you are eating and what your calorie needs are to reach your ideal competitive weight, call a registered dietitian in your area who has worked with athletes to do a nutrient analysis. This will give you an idea if are meeting your calorie intake goals, and the dietitian can also help you to establish an eating plan for reaching your ideal competitive weight. Coaches, you owe it to your athletes to provide the best possible knowledge in every area that affects your gymnasts training. Investing in the expertise of a registered dietitian will benefit both coaches and gymnasts. It is an investment that will ensure the right information is used for reaching and maintaining ideal competitive weight. Remember, optimum performance does not come from dieting. It comes from eating the right foods. Understanding the role that good nutrition plays will enhance your gymnastics experience and be a valuable asset as you pursue excellence.

FOR MORE INFORMATION ON EATING DISORDERS

If you suspect that you, your friend or one of your athletes shows signs of an eating disorder, call the American Dietetic Association at 1-800-366-1655 or (312) 899-0040. They will give you information about facilities in your area that specialize in eating disorders.

References

1. Eisenman, P.A., Johnson, S.C., and Benson, J.E. *Coaches Guide to Nutrition and Weight Control*, 2nd Ed. Champaign, IL: Leisure Press, 1990.
2. Yager, J., Gwirtsman, HE., and Edelstein, CK. *Special Problems in Managing Eating Disorders*. Washington, D.C.: American Psychiatric Press, 1992.
3. Sundgot-Borgen, J. "Prevalence of Eating Disorders in Elite Female Athletes." *International Journal of Sports Nutrition.* 1993;3:29-40.
4. Iverson, Gretchen. "Behind Schedule: Psychosocial Aspects of Delayed Puberty in the Competitive Female Gymnast." *The Sport Psychologist.* 1990;4:155-167.

RECIPES

RECIPE MODIFICATIONS

Some of the most recognizable gymnasts in this country have submitted recipes for this cookbook. I think you'll find it exciting to make the same recipes that are favorites of some of the world's finest gymnasts.

Throughout the recipe chapters, you may find that some of the recipes have been modified. These recipes have been modified to help you as an athlete better meet the dietary standards for gymnastics training. Don't worry, we're showing you the recipes in their original form. These modifications are just suggestions for you to make the recipe better fit your training diet.

Many of the athletes who sent recipes understand that you can include your favorite recipes into your training diet (see next page). They did an excellent job with the recipes they sent in and I think you will be happy with the wide variety of choices you have from this cookbook!

EATING A 20% FAT DIET

After learning about the importance of having a low-fat, high-carbohydrate diet, you must now think that you can never eat foods that are over 20% fat. Wrong! In fact you can most certainly include foods that are higher than 20% fat. The goal is to keep your OVERALL diet at or below 20% fat. Following is an example of a daily diet for a 5-foot, 100 lb. female gymnast, age 14-15. Note that the Designer Turkey Burger (see page 123 for recipe) and Chocolate Angelfood Cake (page 148) is included. Even though the Turkey Burger has 40% of its calories coming from fat, the overall diet is 18% fat. This goes to show that you *can* include some foods that are higher in fat. The key is to choose foods that are very low in fat for the majority of your diet. This will allow some space for those foods that are higher in fat.

Breakfast
1 whole wheat bagel
2 tbsp jam
1 cup nonfat milk
1 medium banana

Lunch
1 turkey breast sandwich (2 slices bread, 3 oz turkey, lettuce, tomato, mustard)
1 medium apple
1 cup nonfat yogurt

Snack
2 oz. Chex corn cereal,dry

Dinner
1 Designer Turkey Burger
1/2 cup potato salad
1 cup diced watermelon
1 cup nonfat milk

Snack/Dessert
1 slice Chocolate Angelfood Cake

Total calories: 2110
Percent calories from:
        Protein: 18%
        Carbohydrates: 64%
        Fat: 18%

So check out the recipes, find your favorites, and include them in your daily diet!

TABLE FOR CONVERSIONS

Volumes
tsp = teaspoon
tbsp = tablespoon
1tsp = 1/3 tbsp
3 tsp = 1 tbsp = 1/2 fluid ounce

2 tbsp = 1/8 cup = 1 fl oz
4 tbsp = 1/4 cup = 2 fl oz
5 1/3 tbsp = 1/3 cup = 2 2/3 fl oz
8 tbsp = 1/2 cup = 4 fl oz
10 2/3 tbsp = 2/3 cup = 5 1/3 fl oz
12 tbsp = 3/4 cup = 6 fl oz
14 tbsp = 7/8 cup = 7 fl oz
16 tbsp = 1 cup = 8 fl oz

1 pint = 2 cups
1 quart = 2 pints
1 gallon = 4 quarts
1 liter = 1.057 quarts

Weights
16 oz = 1 pound (lb)
8 oz = 1/2 lb
4 oz = 1/4 lb

1 oz = 28.4 grams
2.2 lbs = 1 kilogram

CHAPTER 5

BREAKFAST: Great Ways to Start Your Day

Crepes
Tricia Adkins

Gymnastics accomplishments:
-1988, 1989 Rhythmic Group Team member

Recipe received from: A French friend

Recipe:
2-1/2 cups all-purpose flour
6 egg whites
1 tbsp salt
2 cups skim milk
1 cup water

Mix the salt and flour. Add eggs to salt and flour mixture and beat until well mixed. Next, add the milk and water little by little while beating. Let stand for 30 minutes.

Using a Teflon frying pan, spray pan with cooking spray and use high heat, making sure to preheat the pan. Using a small ladle thinly coat the pan, wait until the crepe is slightly brown, (approximately 1-1/2 minutes) and then flip. Pan must be re-sprayed after each crepe.

These crepes can be filled with anything. Roll up and eat while they're hot!

Yields: About 16 crepes

Tips from Michelle: To keep it a low-calorie, low-fat dish, fill with items such as fruit, vegetables, jam, low-fat cottage cheese.

Banana-Nut Muffins
Dominique Dawes

Gymnastics Accomplishments:
-1992 Olympic Team — Barcelona, Spain — 3rd Team, 26th All-Around
-1993 World Championships — Birmingham, England — 4th All-Around
-1994 McDonalds American Cup Champion

Recipe received from: Bisquick™ batter box △

Quote: "Because this recipe is low in cholesterol and fat, it's great anytime (breakfast, lunch, snack)."

Recipe:
  2 cups Bisquick™ pancake mix
  2 egg whites
  1 cup skim milk
  2 bananas, overripe
  2 cups chopped walnuts
  2 tsp sugar

Preheat oven to 375-425 degrees. In a large mixing bowl, add Bisquick. Add egg whites, milk and sugar. Stir until lumps are gone. Add softened bananas and walnuts until they are mixed thoroughly. Pour muffins into muffin tin, and bake for 15 minutes, or until golden brown. If you don't like bananas and walnuts, blueberries can be substituted.

Yields: 12 muffins

Tips from Michelle: The muffin itself is low in fat, but adding the walnuts increases the fat content quite a bit. To decrease the fat, don't use walnuts, or substitute blueberries.

Instead of:
1/2 cup walnuts +
2 bananas

Use:
2 cups blueberries

△Reprinted with the permission of General Mills, Inc.

Ranchero Egg White Omelette
Mary Lou Retton

Gymnastics Accomplishments:
-1984 Olympic All-Around Champion
-1983, 1984, 1985 American Cup Champion
-1983 Chunichi Cup Champion

Recipe received from: My own invention

Quote: "I feel people don't put enough emphasis on breakfast. It's a delicious low-fat dish that makes you feel satisfied."

Recipe:
    5 egg whites
    1/2 cup onion
    1/2 cup green pepper
    1 whole new potato
    1 cup tomato
    1/2 to 1 cup picante sauce
    dash of onion powder
    dash of garlic powder
    dash of black pepper

Chop onion, green pepper, potato and tomato. Separate egg yolks from whites, and place whites in a bowl. Spray nonstick skillet with cooking spray. Heat skillet over medium-high heat. Pan fry onions, green peppers, potatoes and 1/2 cup of tomatoes until warm but crisp (approximately 3-4 minutes). Beat egg whites with a fork, and put egg whites into skillet with the vegetables. Add garlic powder, onion powder and black pepper. Stir egg whites in pan until egg whites are completely cooked. Top with picante sauce and the remaining 1/2 cup of tomatoes.

Note: This dish can be prepared either as an omelette or scrambled, and you can use as little or as much of the seasonings as you like. By adding whole wheat toast to the meal, you can also increase your carbohydrates!

Yields: 1 omelette

Eggs Olé
Bart Conner

Gymnastics Accomplishments:
-1984 Olympic Games — Gold Medal, Team, Parallel Bars
-1979 World Championships — Gold Medal, Parallel Bars
-1975 Pan American Games — Gold Medal, Team

Recipe received from: Mom!

Quote: "My mom makes it and it's great! People are always asking her for the recipe."

Recipe:
　1 dozen eggs
　1/2 pint sour cream
　1/2 stick of margarine
　1 16 oz can stewed tomatoes
　1 green pepper (diced)
　1 pound Velveeta™ Cheese (cubed)
　1 pound ham (cubed)

Preheat oven to 325 degrees. Place tomatoes, green pepper, cheese and ham in a 9" x 13" pan along with 1/2 stick of margarine (cut up and placed throughout the pan). On top, spread evenly 1/2 pint of sour cream. Just before baking, lightly stir 1 dozen eggs in another dish, and pour over items already in the 9" x 13" pan. Bake for 1 hour, or until set.

Yields: 8 servings

Tips from Michelle: This recipe makes my mouth water, but it's fairly high in calories and fat. There are some changes that you can make to this recipe, without changing too much of the original taste and texture.

Instead of:	**Use:**
1 dozen eggs	18 egg whites
1/2 stick of margarine	1/2 stick of light margarine
1/2 pint of sour cream	1/2 pint nonfat yogurt or non-fat sour cream
1 lb of Velveeta™	1/2 lb of part skim mozzarella

Keep all other ingredients the same. By making these changes, you can cut the percentage of calories from fat and total calories in half!

Banana Bread a la Mills
Phoebe Mills

Gymnastics Accomplishments:
-1988 Olympic Bronze Medalist — Balance Beam
-1988 Olympic Trials All-Around Champion
-1988 National All-Around Champion

Quote from Phoebe's mom: "As a gymnast working long hours, Phoebe needed nutritious food with a certain amount of fat and sugar for extra calories and increased energy."

Recipe received from: My mom

Recipe:
1/2 cup butter
1-2/3 cup sugar
2 eggs, slightly beaten
1-1/2 teaspoons baking powder
1/2 teaspoon baking soda
4 tablespoons sour cream
1 cup bananas
2 cups cake flour
1/4 teaspoon salt
1 teaspoon vanilla
1-2 cups chocolate chips

Preheat oven to 350 degrees. In a large bowl, cream butter and sugar with an electric mixer. Add eggs and salt and beat well. In a separate bowl, add baking powder and baking soda to the sour cream, stir well, and add to the egg mixture. Add bananas, then the flour, gradually. Add vanilla, then chocolate chips. Pour batter into a loaf pan (9-1/2" x 5-1/2" x 2-1/2"). Bake at 350° for 1-1/2 hours or until a toothpick, when stuck in the center, comes out clean.

Yields: 8-10 servings

Note: This bread freezes well.

Tips from Michelle: The popularity of bread is really on the "rise," and this recipe is no exception. It is sweet and tasty, but again, those fat calories keep sneaking in there. This recipe does have some good qualities in that some good substitutions can be made.

Instead of:	Use
2 cups chocolate chips	1 cup chocolate chips
1-2/3 cups sugar	1-1/4 cups sugar
4 tbsp sour cream	4 tbsp fat-free sour cream
1/2 cup butter	1/2 cup applesauce

Applesauce works well in place of the butter, and because the applesauce is sweet you can reduce the sugar.

Mom's Waffles for Champions
Chainey Umphrey

Gymnastics Accomplishments:
-1985 Junior National Champion
-1991 USA National Championships — 2nd All-Around
-1993 NCAA National Championships — 2nd All-Around

Recipe received from: Mom Umphrey

Quote: "This recipe keeps your energy level and performance high for a long period of time."

Recipe:
  2 cups whole wheat flour (fresh ground)*
  3 eggs
  1-1/4 cups buttermilk or sweet cream
  1/2 cup peanut oil
  2 tbsp raw honey
  1 tsp sea salt*
  3 tsp baking powder (non-aluminum)*

Add all ingredients in bowl together. Mix. Heat your waffle iron, spray with nonstick cooking spray, and pour mix into iron. Cook until golden brown. Serve with raw honey, jams, fresh fruit or maple syrup.

*Note: Fresh ground whole wheat flour, sea salt, and non-aluminum baking powder can usually be found at health food stores. However, the whole wheat flour, salt and baking powder you find in your supermarket will also work.

Yields: 6 waffles

Tips from Michelle: These waffles are very filling! There are a few changes that you can make to decrease the fat, which is mostly due to the amount of peanut oil used in the original recipe.

Instead of:	Use:
3 eggs	1 egg + 3 egg whites
1/2 cup peanut oil	1/4 cup peanut oil
1-1/4 cup buttermilk/ sweet cream	1-2/3 to 2 cups buttermilk

Chainey's personal recommendations: Drink with lowfat milk. Fresh ground Southern corn grits with a little butter is delicious with this meal as well.

Blueberry Bran Muffins
Sarah Balogach

Gymnastics Accomplishments:
-1990 Jr. Pan American Games — 3rd All-Around, 1st Team
-1992 Olympic Trials competitor
-1992 Pacific Alliance — Seoul, Korea — 12th All-Around, 2nd
 Team

Recipe received from: *Eat to Win* by Dr. Robert Haas Δ

Recipe:
    1-1/4 cups whole wheat flour
    3/4 cup toasted wheat germ
    1-1/2 cups bran
    2 tsp baking powder
    1 tsp baking soda
    1/4 tsp cinnamon
    1 cup apple, shredded, including skins
    1 cup fresh blueberries
    1/3 cup orange juice concentrate
    1 cup granulated fructose
    3/4 cup evaporated skim milk
    3 egg whites

Preheat oven to 350 degrees. Mix all dry ingredients. Add blueberries and apples. Combine all liquid ingredients, and then add to the dry ingredients. Blend well. Spray muffin tin with cooking spray. Fill each tin 2/3 full. Bake 30-35 minutes or until golden brown on top.

Yields: 24 muffins

Δ Reprinted with permission

Breakfast
Analysis Per Serving

Recipe: Crepes
Name: Tricia Adkins

Original
  Calories 83
  Grams of Protein 4.2
  Grams of Carbohydrate 15.4
  Grams of Fat 0.3
  Fiber (grams) 0.5
  Sodium (mg) 466
  % calories from Protein 21%
  % calories from Carbohydrate 76%
  % calories from Fat 3

Recipe: Banana-Nut Muffins
Name: Dominique Dawes

Original
  Calories 241
  Grams of Protein 8.8
  Grams of Carbohydrate 22.7
  Grams of Fat 14.3
  Fiber (grams) 1.7
  Sodium (mg) 186
  % calories from Protein 14%
  % calories from Carbohydrate 36%
  % calories from Fat 50%
Modified
  Calories 96
  Grams of Protein 3.1
  Grams of Carbohydrate 18.8
  Grams of Fat 1.1
  Fiber (grams) 1.0
  Sodium (mg) 187
  % calories from Protein 13%
  % calories from Carbohydrate 77%
  % calories from Fat 10%

Recipe: Ranchero Egg White Omelette
Name: Mary Lou Retton
Original
  Calories 358
  Grams of Protein 24.1
  Grams of Carbohydrate 63.8
  Grams of Fat 2.0
  Fiber (grams) 5.3
  Sodium (mg) 1899
  % calories from Protein 27%
  % calories from Carbohydrate 68%
  % calories from Fat 5%
Special notes on nutrients: Great source of vitamin C from the peppers, onions and tomatoes

Recipe: Eggs Olé
Name: Bart Conner
Original
  Calories 527
  Grams of Protein 34.3
  Grams of Carbohydrate 6.2
  Grams of Fat 40.4
  Fiber (grams) 0.7
  Sodium (mg) 1835
  % calories from Protein 26%
  % calories from Carbohydrate 5%
  % calories from Fat 69%
Modified
  Calories 269
  Grams of Protein 30
  Grams of Carbohydrate 12.4
  Grams of Fat 10.4
  Fiber (grams) 0.7
  Sodium (mg) 1208
  % calories from Protein 46%
  % calories from Carbohydrate 19%
  % calories from Fat 35%
Special notes on nutrients: Great sources of vitamins C, B1, and a good source of B2.

Recipe: Banana Bread a la Mills
Name: Phoebe Mills
Original
Calories 472
Grams of Protein 3.6
Grams of Carbohydrate 74.6
Grams of Fat 19.1
Fiber (grams) .75
Sodium (mg) 283
% calories from Protein 3%
% calories from Carbohydrate 62%
% calories from Fat 35%
Modified
Calories 294
Grams of Protein 3.5
Grams of Carbohydrate 60.5
Grams of Fat 4.7
Fiber (grams) .82
Sodium (mg) 178
% calories from Protein 5%
% calories from Carbohydrate 81%
% calories from Fat 14%

Recipe: Mom's Waffles for Champions
Name: Chainey Umphrey
Original
Calories 384
Grams of Protein 10.1
Grams of Carbohydrate 37
Grams of Fat 22.7
Fiber (grams) 4.3
Sodium (mg) 688
% calories from Protein 10
% calories from Carbohydrate 38
% calories from Fat 52
Modified
Calories 289
Grams of Protein 10.2
Grams of Carbohydrate 37.3
Grams of Fat 11.6
Fiber (grams) 4.3

Sodium (mg) 708
% calories from Protein 14
% calories from Carbohydrate 50
% calories from Fat 36
Special notes on nutrients: Good source of vitamin E

Recipe: Blueberry Bran Muffins
Name: Sarah Balogach

Original
Calories 102
Grams of Protein 4
Grams of Carbohydrate 21
Grams of Fat 1.2
Fiber (grams) N/A
Sodium (mg) 75.1
% calories from Protein 8
% calories from Carbohydrate 82
% calories from Fat 10

SPECIAL NOTE: Analysis from Dr. Robert Haas' book, *Eat To Win*.

CHAPTER 6

SIDE DISHES: The Supporting Cast

Borstsch
Vladimir Artemov

Gymnastics Accomplishments:
-1988 Olympic All-Around Champion (4 golds, 1 silver)
-1983, 1985, 1987, 1989 World Championships
-1983 World University Games — 2nd All-Around, 2nd Floor, 1st
   Team, and Parallel Bars

Recipe received from: Family

Quote: "I like this recipe because it has everything that I need."

Recipe:
3 large potatoes, diced	1/2 lb white onion, chopped
1 lb boneless beef stew, cubed	1/4 lb scallions, chopped
1 lb raw beets, sliced	1 dill pickle, sliced
2 lb (1 large head) raw white cabbage	1 bunch parsley, chopped
1 hot dog, chopped	2 tsp salt
	pepper to taste
	sour cream (optional)

In a large soup pot (at least 6 quarts), put about 4 liters of water. Put beef in water and bring to a boil. Boil for approximately 5 minutes, then reduce heat to a simmer. Add beets and continue to simmer until beets are soft or to desired tenderness. You may then add the rest of the ingredients and continue to simmer for approximately 30-40 minutes. Add salt and pepper. Garnish with sour cream if desired.

Yields: 12 - 2 cup servings

Tips from Michelle: This recipe makes enough to feed the population of a small state! Cut the recipe in half to serve the family. While the water and meat are boiling, you can skim some of the fat off the top. Use fat free sour cream as the garnish.

Oriental Pasta Salad
Jennifer Haase

Gymnastics Accomplishments:
-1989 Rhythmic National Team Member (ranked 5th) -1989
  Rhythmic World Championship Team
-1990 Rhythmic National Team Member (ranked 4th)

Recipe received from: My mother's friend

Quote: "It's fast, transportable, low in calories and great tasting."

Recipe:
1 lb uncooked spaghetti
2 tsp crushed dry red
  pepper
1/4 cup corn oil
1/2 cup sesame oil
5 tbsp soy sauce
6 tbsp honey

1 tsp salt (optional)
1/2 cup chopped cilantro
3/4 cup chopped peanuts
1/2 cup chopped green
  onions
2 tbsp sesame seeds
cilantro leaves for garnish

Cook spaghetti to al dente (tender, but firm) and drain well. In the meantime, in a saucepan, stir red pepper and oils over medium heat for 2 minutes. Add honey, soy sauce and salt. Stir to combine and mix well with cooked spaghetti. Cover and refrigerate for at least 4 hours, or overnight. When ready to serve, add chopped cilantro, peanuts and green onions to noodles. Toss together and place in serving bowl. Sprinkle with sesame seeds and cilantro leaves for garnish. To make this dish into a main dish, add 1 cooked chicken breast (sliced) immediately before serving.

Yields: 8-10 servings

Tips from Michelle: This recipe is great because it adds the spicy oriental flavor with lots of carbohydrates from the pasta. However, the peanuts and oils inflate the fat content. Change a few ingredients, and cut the fat grams in half!

Instead of:
1/4 cup corn oil
1/2 cup sesame oil
3/4 cup peanuts

Use:
2 tbsp corn oil
1/4 cup sesame oil
1/2 cup peanuts

Note: Because you reduce the oils, the crushed red pepper is very strong. You may want to cut back the amount of red pepper you use, unless you like things really hot and spicy!!

Oriental Rice
Heidi Hornbeek

Gymnastics Accomplishments:
-U.S. National Team Member
-Scored two 10.00s at the 1992 Golden Sands Invitational (Bulgaria)
-1992 Chunichi Cup — 4th All-Around

Recipe received from: Mother

Quote: "I love oriental food. Rice is a special favorite of mine."

Recipe:
2 tsp minced ginger
2 large cloves garlic (minced)
1/2 cup defatted chicken stock
3 tbsp lite soy sauce
3 cups sliced mushrooms
2 cups sliced bok choy
1 cup diced bell pepper
1 cup diced carrots
1 cup sliced water chestnuts
4 cups cooked brown rice
1 cup chopped green onions

Saute ginger and garlic in 1/4 cup chicken stock and soy sauce. Add mushrooms, bok choy, bell pepper, carrots, water chestnuts, remaining chicken stock and rice. Cook until vegetables are tender. Add green onion and serve.

Yields: 10 servings

Cabbage Salad
Brandy Johnson-Scharpf

Gymnastics Accomplishments:
-1988 Olympic Team — Highest finisher (men or women)
-1989 World Championship — Silver Medalist (Vault)
-1989 American Cup Champion

Recipe received from: Family

Quote: "Quick, easy to prepare — low calorie and it is very good!"

Recipe:
1 head of cabbage
1 small bunch of green onions
1/2 cup corn oil
6 tbsp rice vinegar
1/4 cup sugar
dash of salt
2 packs Ramen noodles (uncooked)
2 oz almonds
5 tbsp sesame seeds

Slice cabbage thinly. Mix together oil, vinegar, sugar and salt in a small bowl and refrigerate. Cut green onions and mix with sliced cabbage. On a cookie sheet, toast almonds and sesame seeds to a golden brown. Five minutes before serving, lightly toss salad with the refrigerated mixture. Crush the ramen noodles into small pieces and toss into the salad. Add the sesame seeds and almonds and mix.

Yields: 12 servings

Tips from Michelle: This recipe is low in calories, but most of the calories come from fat. On the next page are some suggested changes to cut the fat grams in half.

Instead of:	**Use:**
Regular ramen noodles	Lowfat ramen noodles
1/2 cup corn oil	1/4 cup corn oil
6 tbsp rice vinegar	1/2 cup rice vinegar
2 oz almonds	1 oz almonds

Hot Mediterranean Chicken Salad
Sabrina Mar

Gymnastics Accomplishments:
-1985 U.S. National Champion
-1985, 1987 World Championship Team
-1987 Pan American Games — All-Around Champion

Quote: "I like this because it is relatively low in fat and calories and high in nutritional value."

Recipe:
5 chicken breast halves (trimmed of fat, poached*)
2-1/2 tbsp extra virgin olive oil
1 onion, sliced lengthwise into slivers
1 garlic clove, crushed
1 tbsp chopped fresh oregano (or 1-1/2 tsp dried)
1 cup quartered cherry tomatoes
1/4 cup cooked small green beans
2 tsp grated lemon peel
1 to 2 tbsp white wine vinegar
3 tbsp lemon juice
6 cups finely shredded lettuce
salt, ground pepper to taste
fresh chopped parsley, optional

Remove chicken breasts from poaching liquid and let cool slightly. Remove chicken from bones and tear into medium sized pieces. Set aside. In a large skillet over medium heat, heat olive oil. Add onion and garlic; cook for 2 minutes, stirring constantly. Add oregano. Cook onion mixture for 3 minutes longer until onions are almost transparent, stirring often. Add cherry tomatoes, green beans and lemon peel. Stir until heated through. Add reserved chicken, vinegar, most of lemon juice, and salt and pepper to taste; heat through.

To serve, season shredded lettuce with salt and pepper to taste and remaining lemon juice; divide equally on 6 plates. Spoon hot chicken salad on lettuce and garnish with parsley. Serve immediately.

*To poach chicken, place in deep large skillet and cover with chicken broth. Over medium heat; bring to boil. Reduce heat to low; cover and simmer 15 minutes or until chicken is cooked through.

Yields: 6 servings

Tips from Michelle: Use cooking spray instead of the 2.5 tbsp of olive oil, and lower it to 18% fat calories!

Spinach Salad
Peter Vidmar

Gymnastics Accomplishments:
-1980, 1984 Olympic Team
-1984 Olympic Gold Medalist in Team, Pommel Horse — Silver
   All-Around
-1983, 1984 American Cup Champion

Recipe received from: Wife, Donna

Recipe:
   2 bunches (approximately 8 cups) of fresh spinach
   1/4 cup of wine vinegar
   1/2 cup of sugar
   1/4 tsp paprika
   1 tsp salt
   1/4 cup of oil
   1 tbsp chopped purple onion
   1 tbsp toasted sesame seeds
   bacon bits (approximately 3 tbsp)
   2 hard boiled eggs

Clean spinach, and put in salad bowl. Boil together vinegar, sugar, paprika and salt. Mix vinegar mixture with oil, onion and sesame seeds. Toss salad with bacon bits and egg. Toss with dressing.

Yields: 8-1 cup servings

Tips from Michelle: Again, you can make some substitutions to lower the fat, without losing the flavor. You can cut out 5 g of fat per serving by making a few little changes.

Instead of:	Use:
1/4 cup vinegar	1/2 cup of vinegar
1/4 cup of oil	2 tbsp of oil
2 hard boiled eggs	4 hard boiled egg whites

Fifteen Bean Soup
Tracee Talavera

Gymnastics Accomplishments:
-1980, 1984 Olympic teams
-1979, 1981, 1983 World Championship teams

Recipe received from: Mom

Quote: "I like it because it tastes good and can be served quickly once it is made."

Recipe:
15 bean soup mix package (or any multi-bean soup mix)
1 small onion
1/2 clove garlic
1 large can (16 oz) whole tomatoes, crushed
spices (included in the bean soup mix)

Soak beans for 3-4 hours. Cook beans for 1-1/2 hours at a boil. To make the sauce, fry onions, garlic, and any other vegetable desired (using cooking spray). Add tomatoes to the fry mixture. Add packaged spices. When beans are close to being done, add fried mixture to the beans. Cook for another 1/2 hour at low temperature. Can be served by itself, with cheese on top, or over rice.

Yields: 10 servings

Stir Fry
Hope Spivey-Sheeley

Gymnastics Accomplishments:
-1988 Olympic Team Member
-1991 NCAA All-Around — Vault and Floor Champion
-1991 Honda Sports Award

Quote: "It is a healthy recipe that is also filling."

Recipe received from: I made it up

Recipe:
1 bag of boil-in-the-bag rice
5 sprays canola cooking spray
1 bag (about 16oz) stir fry frozen vegetables
1 tbsp teriyaki sauce
1/8 tsp white pepper
1/8 tsp ground mustard
1/2 tsp Italian seasoning
3 tbsp soy sauce
1 tsp garlic salt
1/2 tsp black pepper

In a skillet or wok, spray canola cooking spray, heat pan, then add rice, and let brown on medium high heat. Be sure to not let it burn. Add 2-1/4 cups of hot water. Add vegetables, and stir. Add seasoning, and stir. Let it come to a boil, reduce heat, cover and simmer until water is absorbed. Stir occasionally. Should be done in 10-15 minutes.

Yields: 5-6 servings

Mexican Dip
Jaycie Phelps

Gymnastics Accomplishments:
-1994 USA Championships — 6th All-Around
-1994 World Championship Trials— 5th All-Around
-1994 World Championships — 2nd Team

Quote: "I like it because I love Mexican food and it's pretty much fat free. I got it from my best friends in Arizona, the Leonards."

Recipe received from: The Leonards

Recipe:
   1 can Frito Lay™ bean dip (14 oz.)
   1 pinto fat free sour cream
   1 envelope taco seasoning (optional)
   1 cup Pace™ picante sauce
   1 bag (16 oz.) baked tortilla chips
   1 small can black olives (optional)

Using an 8 or 9 inch round or square pan, spread the bean dip on the bottom (if using a larger pan, double the ingredients). Mix the sour cream with the package of taco seasoning — stir with a spoon until blended. Spread over the bean dip. Cover that with a layer of picante sauce. Sprinkle sliced black olives over picante sauce. Refrigerate until chilled. Serve with low fat tortilla chips.

Yields: 6-8 servings

Broccoli and Grape Salad
Tom and Lori Forster

Gymnastics Accomplishments:
-Coaches of Kristie Powell, Doni Thompson, Theresa Kulikowski and Kerri Strug
-Coaches at the 1995 Pan American Games, Mar Del Plata, Argentina

Quote: "We like this because it is crunchy and sweet and it's a great new way to eat broccoli."

Recipe received from: "It's homemade."

Recipe:
    6 cups of broccoli, raw
    4 celery spears
    1/2 cup of raisins
    1-1/2 cups grapes
    1 cup fat-free Miracle Whip™

Cut broccoli florets into bite size pieces. Chop celery. Cut grapes into halves. Mix all ingredients with 1 cup (or less) of Miracle Whip™.

Yields: 4 servings

Side Dishes
Analysis Per Serving

Recipe: Stir Fry
Name: Hope Spivey Sheeley
Original
    Calories 108
    Grams of Protein 4.1
    Grams of Carbohydrate 21.7
    Grams of Fat 0.1
    Fiber (grams)
    Sodium (mg) 664
    % calories from Protein 16%
    % calories from Carbohydrate 83%
    % calories from Fat 1%
Special notes on nutrients: Great source of vitamins A and C from veggies

Recipe: Fifteen Bean Soup
Name: Tracee Talavera
Original
    Calories 72
    Grams of Protein 4.4
    Grams of Carbohydrate 12.9
    Grams of Fat .45
    Fiber (grams) 1.8
    Sodium (mg) 139
    % calories from Protein 24%
    % calories from Carbohydrate 71%
    % calories from Fat 5%

Recipe: Spinach Salad
Name: Peter Vidmar
Original
    Calories 152
    Grams of Protein 3.7
    Grams of Carbohydrate 15.4
    Grams of Fat 9.3
    Fiber (grams) 2.2

Sodium (mg) 366
% calories from Protein 9%
% calories from Carbohydrate 39%
% calories from Fat 52%

Modified
Calories 111
Grams of Protein 3.8
Grams of Carbohydrate 16
Grams of Fat 4.3
Fiber (grams) 2.2
Sodium (mg) 373
% calories from Protein 13%
% calories from Carbohydrate 53%
% calories from Fat 34%

Special notes on nutrients: Great sources of vitamin E (from olive oil), and vitamin A and folate from the spinach.

Recipe: Hot Mediterranean Chicken Salad
Name: Sabrina Mar

Original
Calories 236
Grams of Protein 30.2
Grams of Carbohydrate 7.3
Grams of Fat 9.6
Fiber (grams) 1.7
Sodium (mg) 272
% calories from Protein 51%
% calories from Carbohydrate 13%
% calories from Fat 36%

Modified
Calories 187
Grams of Protein 30.2
Grams of Carbohydrate 7.3
Grams of Fat 3.8
Fiber (grams) 1.7
Sodium (mg) 279
% calories from Protein 65%
% calories from Carbohydrate 16%
% calories from Fat 19%

Special notes on nutrients: Great source of niacin and vitamin B6 (from chicken)

Recipe: Cabbage Salad
Name: Brandy Johnson-Scharpf
Original
   Calories 211
   Grams of Protein 3.5
   Grams of Carbohydrate 16.3
   Grams of Fat 15.7
   Fiber (grams) 1.2
   Sodium (mg) 108
   % calories from Protein 6%
   % calories from Carbohydrate 30%
   % calories from Fat 64%
Modified
   Calories 146
   Grams of Protein 3.3
   Grams of Carbohydrate 16.8
   Grams of Fat 8.2
   Fiber (grams) .83
   Sodium (mg) 303
   % calories from Protein 8%
   % calories from Carbohydrate 44%
   % calories from Fat 48%
Special notes on nutrients: Great source of vitamin C from the cabbage and vitamin E from the oil

Recipe: Oriental Rice
Name: Heidi Hornbeek
Original
   Calories 137
   Grams of Protein 4.3
   Grams of Carbohydrate 28
   Grams of Fat 1.1
   Fiber (grams) 3.5
   Sodium (mg) 585
   % calories from Protein 12
   % calories from Carbohydrate 81
   calories from Fat 7
Special notes on nutrients: Great source of vitamin C and A from the vegetables

Recipe: Oriental Pasta Salad
Name: Jennifer Haase
Original
>Calories 399
>Grams of Protein 9.1
>Grams of Carbohydrate 45.2
>Grams of Fat 20.6
>Fiber (grams) 1.8
>Sodium (mg) 780
>% calories from Protein 9%
>% calories from Carbohydrate 45%
>% calories from Fat 46%

Modified
>Calories 316
>Grams of Protein 8.6
>Grams of Carbohydrate 45
>Grams of Fat 11.6
>Fiber (grams) 1.6
>Sodium (mg) 772
>% calories from Protein 11%
>% calories from Carbohydrate 56%
>% calories from Fat 33%

Special notes on nutrients: Great source of vitamin E from the oils

Recipe: Borstsch
Name: Vladimir Artemov
Original
>Calories 177
>Grams of Protein 12.8
>Grams of Carbohydrate 16.8
>Grams of Fat 6.7
>Fiber (grams) 1.1
>Sodium (mg) 606
>% calories from Protein 29%
>% calories from Carbohydrate 37%
>% calories from Fat 34%

Special notes on nutrients: Great source of B12, C and folate

Recipe: Mexican Dip
Name: Jaycie Phelps

Original
   Calories 325
   Grams of Protein 9.2
   Grams of Carbohydrate 60
   Grams of Fat 5.6
   Fiber (grams) 3.7
   Sodium (mg) 700
   % calories from Protein 11%
   % calories from Carbohydrate 73%
   % calories from Fat 16%

Recipe: Broccoli and Grape Salad
Name: Tom and Lori Forster

Original
Calories 164
   Grams of Protein 4.8
   Grams of Carbohydrate 37.3
   Grams of Fat   less than 1
   Fiber (grams) 3.6
   Sodium (mg) 497
   % calories from Protein 11%
   % calories from Carbohydrate 85%
   % calories from Fat 4%

Special notes on nutrients: A great source of vitamin C, vitamin E and folate.

CHAPTER 7

PASTAS, PIZZA AND MORE

Pasta notes: For any of these pasta recipes, be creative and use different types of pastas. Whole wheat pasta is a great choice, because like whole wheat bread, you are getting a better variety of nutrients, including fiber. Try other types as well, such as spinach, or tomato. Also search your specialty food stores for more unique kinds, such as black bean pasta or lemon pepper pasta.

Karyn's "Because I Can't Cook" Macaroni and Cheese
Karyn Lyon Glover

Gymnastics Accomplishments:
-1981 Rhythmic Group World Championships, Munich, Germany
-1983 Rhythmic World Championships, Straussburg, France
-U.S. Rhythmic National Team — 6 years

Recipe from: I made it up

Quote: "It's fast, it's easy, (and) it requires little to no cooking skills."

Recipe:
  1 box of Kraft™ Macaroni and Cheese

Follow the directions on the box — except leave out the butter and milk. Leave one to two tablespoons of water when draining the noodles. Throw in the cheese, and mix it up. It tastes just about the same and you will avoid some of the extra fat.

Yields: 2 servings

Lowfat Lasagna
Hilary Grivich

Gymnastics Accomplishments:
-1990 Junior National Champion
-1991 USA vs. Romania — 3rd All-Around
-1991 World Championship Team — 2nd Team

Quote: "This recipe is an excellent source of energy, and it's low in fat."

Recipe received from: My mom

Recipe:
15 oz (1 carton) lowfat ricotta or cottage cheese, well drained
1 egg (optional)
1 tsp Italian seasoning
1 to 1-1/2 lb low fat ground turkey, browned and drained
32 oz jar of spaghetti sauce
9 dry lasagna noodles
16 oz shredded low fat mozzarella cheese
1/4 cup grated parmesan cheese (optional)

In a small bowl, combine ricotta cheese, egg and seasoning; set aside. Brown ground turkey and add to spaghetti sauce; mix well. To make 3 layer lasagna, evenly spread 1 cup of spaghetti sauce mixture into bottom of ungreased 9" x 13" x 2" glass baking dish. Cover with 3 dry lasagna noodles. Do not allow noodles to touch outer edges of dish. Cover noodles with 1 cup of sauce, covering noodles completely. Layer 1/2 of ricotta cheese mixture and 1/3 of mozzarella cheese on top of sauce. Repeat layers of noodles, sauces and cheeses two more times, ending with shredded mozzarella cheese on top. Sprinkle with parmesan cheese if desired.

For microwave oven: Cover with plastic wrap. Cook on high power for 17-19 minutes, turning dish twice during cooking. Let stand 5 minutes before cutting and serving.

For conventional oven: Preheat oven to 350° degrees. Cover with aluminum foil and bake for 30-40 minutes. To brown cheese, uncover dish during last 10-15 minutes of baking. Let stand 5 minutes before cutting and serving.

Yields: 6-8 servings

Notes: Lasagna can be made ahead of time and frozen. To microwave, cook frozen lasagna on defrost for 18-20 minutes, then proceed as directed above. For conventional oven, bake an additional 20-30 minutes.

Tips from Michelle: This is a great modified dish, considering that regular lasagna can have upwards of 50% of its calories from fat. If you want to go even lower in fat and calories, cut down on the meat and cheese that you use. By reducing the meat and cheeses by 25%, and by using nonfat cottage cheese, calories from fat will drop to 34%.

Instead of:	Use:
1 lb ground turkey	3/4 lb ground turkey
1 lb mozzarella cheese	3/4 lb mozzarella cheese

Mostacciolli
Martha Grubbs

Gymnastics Accomplishments:
-1993 Senior National Team Member
-1993 U.S. Classic — 5th All-Around
-South African Cup — 2nd All-Around

Quote: "I like pasta a lot, but most of all I like mostaccioli because it's a good carbohydrate and it tastes great!"

Recipe received from: My mother

Recipe:
1/4 lb dried mushrooms
1 tbsp butter
3/4 to 1 lb ground round steak
1 large chopped onion
1 clove garlic, cut into halves
3/4 tsp salt
1/8 tsp pepper
2 cups canned tomatoes
1/2 tsp basil
1/2 tsp oregano
1/4 cup olive oil
1/2 lb uncooked mostaccioli
grated parmesan cheese

Reconstitute 1/4 lb dried mushrooms. Melt 1 tbsp butter and add ground round steak, stirring until brown. Add chopped onion and garlic. Cover these ingredients with boiling water. Add in salt and pepper. Simmer covered until almost dry. Take out the garlic clove and add canned tomatoes, basil and oregano. Continue to simmer, stirring frequently. Cook until the sauce is thick (about 1 to 1-1/2 hours). As it thickens, add mushrooms, and when the sauce is almost done add olive oil. In a separate pan, boil mostaccioli in salted water until tender. Serve the mostaccioli on a hot platter; first a layer of pasta and then a layer of sauce, then a layer of pasta and then again a layer of sauce. Sprinkle each meat sauce layer generously with grated parmesan cheese and pepper.

Yields: 5 servings

Tips from Michelle: This is a great pasta dish! Use a lean ground beef, and cut out the unneccesary fats (butter, olive oil), because even lean meat has enough fat for cooking.

Eliminate: butter and olive oil

Spaghetti Vesuvio
Kathy Johnson-Clarke

Gymnastics Accomplishments:
-1980, 1984 Olympic Team Member and Captain
-1984 Olympic Games — Silver medal (Team), Bronze medal (Balance Beam)
-1978 World Championships — Bronze medalist (Floor)

Quote: "I love pasta for the taste and the complex carbohydrates for energy. Italian plum tomatoes make my favorite sauce and I get a little protein with a small amount of fat from the mozzarella cheese. It's great with a green salad with Italian or oil and vinegar dressing. And it's quick and easy."

Recipe received from: *Top 100 Pasta Sauces* Δ

Recipe:
1 lb uncooked spaghetti
1 tbsp olive oil
28 oz Italian plum tomatoes
1 tsp dried oregano
salt or garlic salt to taste
2 oz freshly grated parmesan cheese
7 oz mozzarella cheese

Warm the oil in a pan and add the tomatoes (in their juice), squashing them with a fork. Add the oregano and salt (or garlic salt) to taste and cook rapidly (over higher heat) for 20 minutes. While the sauce is cooking, chop the mozzarella into small cubes. Cook the pasta by following the directions on the pasta package, being careful to avoid overcooking. When the pasta is ready, drain and add the freshly grated parmesan, the tomato sauce and the diced mozzarella. Toss rapidly, then cover for about three minutes so that the mozzarella begins to melt and look like streams of molten lava. Serve hot.

Yields: 7-8 servings

Δ"Spaghetti Vesuvio" excerpted from *Top 100 Pasta Sauces* by Diane Seed. Copyright D 1987 by Diane Seed. Used by permission of Ten Speed Press, P.O. Box 7123, Berkeley, CA 94707.

Spaghetti Iolia
Dominick Minicucci

Gymnastics Accomplishments
-1988 Olympic Team
-1992 Olympic Team
-1984 Junior National Class II Champion

Quote: "It's delicious! And it is a tradition to eat Spaghetti Iolia in my family every Friday night."

Recipe received from: My father

Recipe:
    1/4 cup olive oil
    1 clove garlic (fresh)
    1 medium zucchini
    1 lb uncooked spaghetti
    1 cup water
    grated cheese, salt and pepper (optional)

In a large pot, bring about 2 quarts of water to a boil. Cook spaghetti to desired tenderness. While water is boiling, slice zucchini into thin slices. In a frying pan, add olive oil (to cover bottom of pan). Fry zucchini (over low flame) until golden brown — place on a paper towel to drain excess oil. Next, dice garlic into small pieces. In the same frying pan, brown garlic (over low flame, making sure not to overcook). Turn off stove — add 1 cup of water to the garlic in the frying pan. Drain spaghetti and pour garlic, oil and water mixture over it. Add the zucchini and mix together in a large bowl.

Yields: 5-6 servings

Note: Grated cheese, salt and pepper can be added if desired.

Tips from Michelle: Use 1/2 the oil for frying, and cut 10% of the fat calories

Instead of:	Use:
1/4 cup olive oil	1/8 cup (4 tbsp) olive oil

Peanut Sauce Linguini
Marie Roethlisberger

Gymnastics Accomplishments:
-1984 Olympic Team
-1985 World Championship Team
-1983 World Championship Team

Quote: "I'm Italian and love pasta! This is a new one I just got my hands on."

Recipe received from: A friend

Recipe:
    10 oz linguini pasta
    1/4 cup peanut butter
    3 tbsp sugar
    1/4 cup soy sauce (or tamari sauce)
    1 tsp red pepper flakes
    3 tbsp sesame oil
    3 tbsp vegetable oil
    1 tbsp garlic (minced)
    2 tsp ginger
    4 medium peppers (raw)
    1 cup thinly sliced carrots (raw)

Cook pasta until tender. Mix together peanut butter, sugar, soy sauce, pepper flakes, sesame oil, vegetable oil and garlic. In a frying pan, spray with cooking spray and saute ginger, carrots and peppers. Add peanut butter mixture to the frying pan and heat through. Combine with pasta and serve.

Yields: 4 servings

Tips from Michelle: You can experiment with the vegetables that you use, and the more colorful the better in this spicy dish. A couple of changes that you can make to lower the fat include:

Instead of:	**Use:**
3 tbsp vegetable oil	No vegetable oil
1/4 cup (4 tbsp) peanut butter	3 tbsp peanut butter

By taking out the vegetable oil, but keeping the sesame oil in, you can retain the oriental quality of the dish. Peanut butter makes this dish taste wonderful, but it also adds a lot of fat. By removing 1 tbsp you can reduce the fat but not the peanut butter flavor.

Garlic and Broccoli Pasta
Valerie Zimring

Gymnastics Accomplishments:
-1984 Olympic Rhythmic Gymnastics Team
-1984 National Rhythmic All-Around Champion
-1981, 1983 World Championship Team member

Quote: "This is a super easy and wonderfully delicious recipe that requires little advanced preparation. You can make as little or as much as you want and vary the ingredient amounts to your individual taste. I like to serve this dish with a large salad of baby lettuce and tomatoes. Enjoy!"

Recipe received from: My sister Lori (she created it)

Recipe:
   2 bunches broccoli
   1/2 cup olive oil
   4 large cloves of garlic
   1/2 cup parmesan cheese
   black pepper to taste
   1 lb uncooked pasta, any style

Put a large stock pot, 2/3 full with water, on boil. Cut broccoli into large florets and wash. When water comes to a full boil add pasta and stir. Add broccoli and cover. Stir occasionally. On stove, saute garlic in olive oil.* Saute until garlic just begins to brown. Set aside. Test pasta for desired tenderness and drain, with broccoli, and return to pot or serving bowl. Pour garlic and oil mixture onto broccoli and pasta and stir together (broccoli will crumble and mix with pasta). Add parmesan cheese and mix (drizzle extra olive oil if too dry). Add pepper to taste and serve.

Yields: 4 servings

*Always heat pan slightly before adding olive oil, and heat oil slightly before adding garlic.

Tips from Michelle: As Valerie said, this dish is very adaptable and you can use more or less of any of the ingredients. This dish does turn out well with less olive oil and parmesan cheese, thereby reducing the fat calories and letting you enjoy the taste of the garlic and broccoli.

Instead of:	Use:
1/2 cup olive oil	1/4 cup olive oil
1/2 cup parmesan	1/3 cup parmesan

Deepdish Vegetarian Pizza
Tim LaFleur

Gymnastics Accomplishments:
-1979 World Championships, Bronze Medalist (Team)
-1978 Nissen Award Winner
-3 time Big Ten All-Around Champion

Quote: "It tastes good, it's easy to make and it's good for you."

Recipe received from: Peter Shapiro

Recipe:
2 packages of dry, prepackaged pizza crust mix
1 small can (4 oz) tomato paste (optional)
3 tomatoes, sliced
1 cup of mushrooms, sliced
1-2 avocados, sliced
1 onion, chopped
1/2 green pepper, chopped
2 lb mozzarella, thinly sliced or shredded
1 can large black olives, sliced
oregano, garlic, pepper, salt to taste
1 pkg pepperoni slices (optional)

Preheat oven to 350°. Prepare pizza crust mix as directed. Spread dough in an ungreased 9" x 12" cake pan, spreading dough up the sides of the pan. Spread a thin layer of tomato paste on the bottom of the crust. Layer the vegetables, starting with the tomato slices and ending with a layer of mozzarella cheese. You can usually get 2-3 layers in the pan, depending on the number and thickness of the ingredients. Add a layer of spices to taste on top of each layer. End with a layer of mozzarella cheese. Bake approximately 25 minutes at 350° or until the crust and cheese are browned. Allow 5 minutes to cool and then cut into 10-12 slices.

Yields: 10-12 slices for each pizza

Except for the tomatoes and onions, any of the vegetables can be deleted. You can also add other vegetables such as finely chopped broccoli. Pepperoni can also be added to each layer if desired (for the nonvegetarian version).

Tips from Michelle: For all of you pizza lovers, this is for you! Pizza can be a healthy meal. Vegetarian pizza is the best choice for a low-fat dish, but you also must be careful of those non-meat items that are high in fat. Avocados and olives, although vegetables, are fat traps.

Instead of:	Use:
Avocado	broccoli
olives	omit olives
2 lb cheese	1 lb cheese

These changes can make pizza a possibility in a low-fat meal plan!

Pasta Analysis Per Serving

Recipe: "Because I Can't Cook" Macaroni and Cheese
Name: Karyn Lyon Glover

Original
  Calories 380
  Grams of Protein 18
  Grams of Carbohydrate 72
  Grams of Fat 4
  Fiber (grams) N/A
  Sodium (mg) 420
  % calories from Protein 18
  % calories from Carbohydrate 73
  % calories from Fat 9

Recipe: Lowfat Lasagna
Name: Hilary Grivich

Original
  Calories 514
  Grams of Protein 42
  Grams of Carbohydrate 39
  Grams of Fat 22
  Fiber (grams) 1.5
  Sodium (mg) 1107
  % calories from Protein 32
  % calories from Carbohydrate 30
  % calories from Fat 38
Modified
  Calories 450
  Grams of Protein 35
  Grams of Carbohydrate 40
  Grams of Fat 17
  Fiber (grams) 1.5
  Sodium (mg) 1033
  % calories from Protein 31

% calories from Carbohydrate 35
% calories from Fat 34

Special notes on nutrients: Good vitamin C and B12 source (from sauce and lean turkey, respectfully). Also a great source of vitamin A from cheese.

Recipe: Mostacciolli
Name: Martha Grubbs

Original
  Calories 522
  Grams of Protein 25
  Grams of Carbohydrate 41
  Grams of Fat 28
  Fiber (grams) 3.2
  Sodium (mg) 606
  % calories from Protein 19
  % calories from Carbohydrate 32
  % calories from Fat 49

Modified
  Calories 399
  Grams of Protein 25
  Grams of Carbohydrate 41
  Grams of Fat 14.4
  Fiber (grams) 3.2
  Sodium (mg) 582
  % calories from Protein 25
  % calories from Carbohydrate 42
  % calories from Fat 33

Special notes on nutrients: Great source of vitamin B12 and niacin from the lean beef, and good source of vitamin C from the tomato sauce.

Recipe: Spaghetti Vesuvio
Name: Kathy Johnson - Clarke

Original
  Calories 348
  Grams of Protein 18.5
  Grams of Carbohydrate 46.6
  Grams of Fat 9.3
  Fiber (grams) 2.5
  Sodium (mg) 745
  % calories from Protein 22

% calories from Carbohydrate 54
% calories from Fat 24
Special notes on nutrients: Good source of calcium from cheese
and vitamin C from the tomatoes

Recipe: Spaghetti Iolia
Name: Dominick Minicucci
Original
   Calories 368
   Grams of Protein 10.9
   Grams of Carbohydrate 55.3
   Grams of Fat 10.8
   Fiber (grams) 2.8
   Sodium (mg) 7.5
   % calories from Protein 12
   % calories from Carbohydrate 61
   % calories from Fat 27
Modified
   Calories 325
   Grams of Protein 10.9
   Grams of Carbohydrate 55.3
   Grams of Fat 6.1
   Fiber (grams) 2.8
   Sodium (mg) 7.5
   % calories from Protein 14
   % calories from Carbohydrate 69
   % calories from Fat 17
Special notes on nutrients: Good source of B1 from pasta and
vitamin E from olive oil

Recipe: Peanut Sauce Linguini
Name: Marie Roethlisberger
Original
   Calories 614
   Grams of Protein 16.5
   Grams of Carbohydrate 72.5
   Grams of Fat 31
   Fiber (grams) 5.2
   Sodium (mg) 1084
   % calories from Protein 10
   % calories from Carbohydrate 46
   % calories from Fat 44

Modified
  Calories 503
  Grams of Protein 15.5
  Grams of Carbohydrate 71.8
  Grams of Fat 18.5
  Fiber (grams) 4.9
  Sodium (mg) 1080
  % calories from Protein 12
  % calories from Carbohydrate 56
  % calories from Fat 32

Special notes on nutrients: Great source of vitamin A from carrots, vitamin C from the peppers and B1 from the pasta

Recipe: Garlic and Broccoli Pasta
Name: Valerie Zimring

Original
  Calories 760
  Grams of Protein 24.5
  Grams of Carbohydrate 90.3
  Grams of Fat 33.8
  Fiber (grams) 4.7
  Sodium (mg) 242
  % calories from Protein 13
  % calories from Carbohydrate 47
  % calories from Fat 40

Modified
  Calories 619
  Grams of Protein 23
  Grams of Carbohydrate 90.3
  Grams of Fat 18.7
  Fiber (grams) 4.7
  Sodium (mg) 177
  % calories from Protein 15
  % calories from Carbohydrate 58
  % calories from Fat 27

Special notes on nutrients: Great vitamin C source and folate source from broccoli

Recipe: Deepdish Vegetarian Pizza
Name: Tim LaFleur

Original
  Calories 215
  Grams of Protein 13
  Grams of Carbohydrate 18.6
  Grams of Fat 9.9
  Fiber (grams) 1.0
  Sodium (mg) 331
  % calories from Protein 24
  % calories from Carbohydrate 36
  % calories from Fat 41
Modified
  Calories 144
  Grams of Protein 7.9
  Grams of Carbohydrate 17.8
  Grams of Fat 4.7
  Fiber (grams) 0.9
  Sodium (mg) 202
  % calories from Protein 22
  % calories from Carbohydrate 50
  % calories from Fat 28
Special notes on nutrients: Good calcium source from the
cheese. The modified version is a great source of vitamin C
from the broccoli, and a great source of vitamin B2 from the
crust

CHAPTER 8

MEAT AND POULTRY:
Protein Perfection

Designer Turkey Burgers
Robyn Barnes

Gymnastics Accomplishments:
-1989 Rhythmic National Group Team, World Championships
   Team
-1989 Illinois State Ribbon Champion — Class I Elite
-1987 Class II Nationals — 4th AA

Quote: "It's easy to make and tastes great."

Recipe received from: A newspaper article

Recipe:
   1 lb ground turkey
   1 tsp chicken bouillon granules
   3/8 cup lite ranch dressing
   2 tbsp minced shallots
   1/4 cup finely grated carrot
   1/4 tsp dried tarragon
   1/4 tsp black pepper
   4 sourdough rolls
   1 cup alfalfa sprouts
   1 small tomato, sliced

Combine turkey with bouillon granules, 1/8 cup ranch dressing and vegetables, herbs and seasonings. Mix. Shape into 4 patties. Bake about 15 minutes at 350° or grill. Put on sourdough rolls, top with tomato and sprouts and drizzle with remaining 1/4 cup ranch dressing. Serve hot.

Yields: 4 burgers

Chicken and Long Rice
Lydia Bree

Gymnastics Accomplishments:
-1982 National Champion and Gymnast of the Year
-4 time World Championship Team Member
-1984 Olympic Team alternate

Quote: "Chicken and Long Rice is satisfying and fun to eat. I enjoy a wide variety of ethnic foods so this fits in nicely."

Recipe received from: A Phillipino friend

Recipe:
2 cups chicken, chopped in bite size pieces
2 tbsp margarine
4 carrots, peeled and sliced
1 onion, cut in strips
3 pieces of celery, sliced
2 cups long grain rice, uncooked
1/2 head cabbage, cut in small pieces
3 tbsp soy sauce
salt, pepper, garlic salt to taste

Cook chicken. Skin, bone and cut into bite size pieces. Stir fry carrots, onion, and celery in margarine. Add chicken, soy sauce and spices. Stir together and remove from heat. Place long rice in a large pot and cover with boiling water. Let soak until tender. Add chicken and vegetables. Bring to a boil. Add cabbage and cover. Turn off heat and let cabbage steam until tender (about 5 minutes). Stir and serve

Yields: 6 servings

Chicken and Rice Surprise
Kelly Garrison

Gymnastics Accomplishments:
-1988 U.S. Olympic Team and Team Captain
-Three skills on Balance Beam named Garrison
-First woman to score 10.00 in NCAA Competition

Quote: "(This recipe is) low-cal and yummy, great during training."

Recipe received from: Coach Becky Buwick

Recipe:
2-1/4 cups Minute Rice,™ uncooked
1 can cream of chicken soup
milk,* measured to 1/2 of the soup can
water, measured to 1/2 of the soup can
4 boneless, skinless chicken breasts

Preheat oven to 375 degrees. Put 2-1/4 cups of Minute Rice™ in a 3 quart dish. Mix 1 can of cream of chicken soup, 1/2 soup can of milk and 1/2 soup can of water together and pour onto rice. Stir rice until completely coated. Place 4 chicken breasts on rice and stir rice mixture to cover breasts slightly. Bake with lid on 375° for 45 minutes. Check occasionally to make sure there is plenty of liquid. If dry, add water or milk and stir.

Yields: 4 servings

*May substitute water for milk

Santa Fe Grilled Chicken Breasts
Caroline Hunt

Gymnastics Accomplishments:
-1992 Rhythmic World Championship Team Member
-1992 Rhythmic Olympic Trials — 5th All-Around

Quote: "I like grilled chicken, and the homemade salsa tastes fresh."

Recipe received from: *Cooking Light 1991* Δ

Recipe:
4 skinless, boneless chicken
  breasts (4 oz each)
1/4 tsp salt
1/4 tsp pepper
1/3 cup lime juice
2 tsp olive oil
1-3/4 cup diced plum tomatoes

1/3 cup chopped onion
3 tbsp fresh cilantro,
  minced
2 tbsp red wine vinegar
1 tbsp minced jalapeno
  pepper
vegetable cooking spray

Flatten chicken breasts (with a meat tenderizer) until chicken breasts are 1/2" thick. Make 1/8" diagonal slits across each breast, making a diamond pattern. Sprinkle breasts with salt and pepper - place in a shallow bowl. Combine lime juice and olive oil, stir, pour over chicken, and marinate in refrigerator for 3 hours. Combine tomato with the next 4 ingredients and stir. Cover and chill well. Remove chicken from marinade. Coat grill with cooking spray, and grill each chicken breast for 5 minutes on each side over medium hot coals. Cut chicken into thin slices, and top with tomato mixture. You can also serve the chicken on top of a bed of lettuce as a chicken salad.

Yields: 4 servings

Δ Reprinted with permission from Oxmoor House publishing.

Chicken Risotto
Valeri Liukin

Gymnastics Accomplishments:
-1988 Olympic Gold Medalist — High bar, team
-1988 Olympic Bronze Medalist — All-Around
-1987, 1991 World Champion

Quote: "It's really delicious."

Recipe:
2 sprigs of parsley
1 medium onion
1 red pepper
2 tbsp olive oil
4 oz button mushrooms
4 oz peas
12 oz chicken, cooked
12 oz long grain rice (about 1-7/8 cup)
1 tbsp chili sauce
salt and black pepper
lemon twists

First, cook rice, following directions on package. Next, chop finely the onion, parsley, and pepper. Heat the oil in a pan and fry the chopped onion and pepper until soft. Slice the mushrooms, add to the onions and fry for 2 minutes more. Add the chopped parsley, peas, diced chicken, cooked rice and chili sauce, and season to taste. Fry gently to reheat, about 15 minutes. Garnish with lemon twists and parsley sprigs.

Yields: 4 servings

Tips from Michelle: As in many of the other recipes that we have discussed, you can decrease your frying oil, reducing the fat. Try 2 tsp of oil instead of 2 tbsp.

Special tip from Valeri: Always smile while you're cooking!!

Crock Pot Roast
Shannon Miller

Gymnastics Accomplishments:
-1992 Olympic Games -Silver — All-Around, Bars. Bronze —
   Team, Balance, Beam, Floor
-1993 World Champion — All-Around
-1994 World Champion — All-Around, Balance Beam

Quote: "It's nutritious (meat and vegetables) and it tastes great, plus it's so easy to make."

Recipe received from: My mother

Recipe:
   2 large potatoes
   5 to 6 carrots
   1 onion (optional)
   2 spears celery (optional)
   2 to 3 lb roast (any kind, such as chuck, arm, rump)
   1 cup water

Scrape and chop carrots. One inch size works well. Peel and cut potatoes into medium size chunks (leave skin on potatoes if you like). Place roast on top of carrots and potatoes (celery can be chopped up and added to carrots and potatoes). Slice onion on top of roast. Add salt and pepper to taste. Pour in one cup of water. Turn crock pot on HIGH. Cook a minimum of 5 hours or leave in up to 6 hours. Juice remaining after meat and vegetables have been removed can be used to make gravy.

Yields: 5 servings

Tips from Michelle: This recipe proves that you can use beef to produce a healthy dish that's not too high in fat. You must choose your beef carefully, however, and go for the leaner cuts. In this recipe, the rump roast works best and is lowest in fat. It may need to be cooked to 6 hours, however, because it is a tougher meat.

Hawaiian Chicken
Monica Shaw

Gymnastics Accomplishments:
-1992 USA Championships — 15th All-Around
-1992 Puerto Rico Cup — 2nd All-Around, 1st Uneven Bars
-1992 Chunichi Cup — 10 All-Around, 2nd Uneven Bars

Quote: "It is very good! It is low in fat grams and very high in carbohydrates which is what all gymnasts are watching all the time."

Recipe received from: My mother, (a family recipe)

Recipe:

1-1/2 lb chicken breast
flour
salt
cooking oil (or spray)
1 can (15-1/2 oz) pineapple
  chunks
1/2 cup honey
2 tbsp cornstarch
3/4 cup vinegar

1 tbsp soy sauce
1/4 tsp ginger
1 chicken bouillon cube
1 green pepper (cut in 1/4"
  strips)
1/4 cup coarsely grated
  carrot
cooked rice

Roll chicken pieces in flour and sprinkle with salt. Brown chicken in an oiled, heated fry pan. Drain pineapple; reserve pineapple chunks, and pour juice into measuring cup. Add water to make 1-1/2 cups. Add honey, cornstarch, vinegar, soy sauce, ginger and bouillon cube. Bring to a boil and boil 2 minutes, stirring constantly. Pour over chicken pieces in 2-quart baking dish. Bake at 350 degrees, uncovered for 30 minutes. Add pineapple chunks and green pepper. Bake 30 minutes longer or until chicken is tender. Serve with cooked rice.

Yields: 6 servings

Honey Glazed Chicken Breasts
Simona Soloveychik

Gymnastics Accomplishments:
-1985 Rhythmic World Championships Team
-1986 Four Continent Championships

Quote: "It's quick, easy, few ingredients and very versatile."

Recipe received from: A friend

Recipe:
    4 chicken breasts
    1/4 cup teriyaki sauce (you may also use lite)
    1/2 cup honey

Preheat oven to 375° degrees. Place chicken breasts in an aluminum foil-lined baking tray and sprinkle lightly with teriyaki sauce. Cover with foil and bake at 350-375° for 20-25 minutes, or until chicken begins to brown. Pour honey over chicken and cover with foil again. Finish cooking (approximately another 20 minutes). You may want to remove the foil for the last 5 minutes of cooking so that the chicken will brown.

Yields: 4 servings

Notes from Simona: These are great plain or on a sandwich with lettuce and tomato. You can also dice chicken and toss with a salad. ENJOY!

Slow Cooker Chicken and Vegetables
Kim Stiles

Gymnastics Accomplishments:
-7 time Rhythmic National Team Member
-2 time Rhythmic World Championship Team Member
-Switzerland Group Team Invitational — 3rd Team

Quote: "(I like this recipe) because it's healthy and good to eat. Because it is a slow cooker, it is nice to put it all together in the morning and then leave it until dinner time because it is a one dish meal."

Recipe received from: My mom

Recipe:
2 medium onions, coarsely chopped

8 medium carrots, cut into 1/2" slices

4 celery spears, chopped

3 cups frozen hash browns (about 1 lb)

1 cup frozen corn kernels

1 can (4oz) mushrooms, stems and pieces

1-1/2 lb skinless, boneless chicken breasts, cut into 1" chunks

2 cans (10-3/4 oz each) condensed golden mushroom soup

1/4 cup dry white wine

1/2 tsp pepper

1 package (16oz) frozen peas — thawed

Turn a 6 quart electric crockery-cooker on high heat setting while preparing ingredients. In crockery pot, combine onions, carrots, celery, potatoes, corn, mushrooms, chicken, undiluted soup, wine, and pepper. Mix well. Cover, reduce heat to low, and cook for 5-1/2 hours. Stir in peas, cover and cook for another 1/2 hour. Uncover and cook an extra 15 minutes.

Yields: 8 servings

Tips from Michelle: Reduce some of the fat by making two changes:

Instead of:	Use:
2 cans condensed mushroom soup	1 can condensed mushroom soup + 1/2 cup nonfat milk
3 cups hash browns	2 cups hash browns

Cabbage Chicken
Kim Zmeskal

Gymnastics Accomplishments:
-1991 World All-Around Champion, 1992 World Champion —
   Beam, Floor
-1990, 1991, 1992 National Champion
-1992 Olympic Team — Bronze medal (Team)

Quote: "This recipe tastes great, it's light and Mom says it's quick and easy to make."

Recipe received from: Mom

Recipe:
   6-8 skinless, boneless chicken breasts
   1 small or 1/2 large head of cabbage
   1 can (20 oz) chunky pineapple
   3 tbsp soy sauce
   dash of salt
   1 tsp pepper
   1 tbsp margarine
   3 cups cooked rice

Cut up chicken breast into bite size pieces. Season lightly with salt and pepper. Sauté chicken in 1 tbsp margarine or butter in large frying pan or Dutch oven. Chop cabbage into chunky pieces and stir into chicken. Add soy sauce and drained pineapple chunks to mixture. Cover and let steam until tender (approximately 5-10 minutes) on medium to low heat. Thicken the juices of the mixture by mixing 1 tbsp cornstarch with a little cold water until smooth, and then mix into the juices of the chicken/cabbage mixture. Serve with 1/2 cup cooked rice for each serving.

Variation: If you like, add 1 chopped onion and bell pepper as you sauté chicken.

Yields: 6 servings

Chicken Mozzarella
Kerri Strug

Gymnastics Accomplishments:
-1992 Olympic Team — Bronze medal (Team)
-1991 World Championships — 2nd Team
-1992, 1993, 1994, 1995 World Championships Team member

Quote: "(I like this) because it tastes like Chicken Parmesan, but it is very low in fat."

Recipe received from: My friend Marianna Webster

Recipe:
4 whole boneless, skinless chicken breasts (4 oz each)
2 cups corn flakes, crushed
2 egg whites, slightly beaten
16 oz jar low fat spaghetti sauce
1 cup fat free mozzarella cheese, shredded
1/4 cup water

Preheat oven to 350°. Dip chicken breasts in egg whites, roll in corn flakes and place in large skillet sprayed with non-stick cooking spray. Brown on both sides. Spray a shallow baking dish with cooking spray and place chicken breasts in dish. Mix water with spaghetti sauce and pour over chicken breasts. Cover top with shredded fat free mozzarella cheese and bake at 350° for 35-40 minutes.

Yields: 4 servings

Meat and Poultry Analysis Per Serving

Recipe: Designer Turkey Burgers

Name: Robyn Barnes

Original

    Calories 416

    Grams of Protein 29.8

    Grams of Carbohydrate 34.0

    Grams of Fat 18.7

    Fiber (grams) .84

    Sodium (mg) 865

    % calories from Protein 28

    % calories from Carbohydrate 32

    % calories from Fat 40

Special notes on nutrients: Good source of zinc, and a great source of vitamin E and vitamin A.

Recipe: Chicken and Long Rice

Name: Lydia Bree

Original

    Calories 409

    Grams of Protein 19.7

    Grams of Carbohydrate 63.3

    Grams of Fat 7.6

    Fiber (grams) 3.0

    Sodium (mg) 1402

    % calories from Protein 20

    % calories from Carbohydrate 64

    % calories from Fat 16

Special notes on nutrients: Great source of niacin, vitamin A and vitamin E

Recipe: Chicken and Rice Surprise
Name: Kelly Garrison
Original
   Calories 443
   Grams of Protein 32.8
   Grams of Carbohydrate 55.3
   Grams of Fat 8.6
   Fiber (grams) 1.7
   Sodium (mg) 1274
   % calories from Protein 31
   % calories from Carbohydrate 51
   % calories from Fat 18
Special notes on nutrients: Great source of niacin, vitamin B6, and a good source of thiamin (B1)

Recipe: Santa Fe Grilled Chicken Breast
Name: Caroline Hunt
Original
   Calories 224
   Grams of Protein 34.8
   Grams of Carbohydrate 4.2
   Grams of Fat 6.3
   Fiber (grams) .40
   Sodium (mg) 238
   % calories from Protein 65
   % calories from Carbohydrate 8
   % calories from Fat 27
Special notes on nutrients: Great source of niacin, vitamin B6 and a good source of vitamin C

Recipe: Chicken Risotto
Name: Valerie Liukin
Original
   Calories 573
   Grams of Protein 33
   Grams of Carbohydrate 78
   Grams of Fat 13.9
   Fiber (grams) 3.3
   Sodium (mg) 232
   % calories from Protein 23

% calories from Carbohydrate 55
% calories from Fat 22
Special notes on nutrients: Great source of niacin, vitamin C and a good source of vitamin B6

Recipe: Crock Pot Roast
Name: Shannon Miller
Original
  Calories 452
  Grams of Protein 53.6
  Grams of Carbohydrate 24.6
  Grams of Fat 11.9
  Fiber (grams) 1.4
  Sodium (mg) 139
  % calories from Protein 51
  % calories from Carbohydrate 23
  % calories from Fat 26
Special notes on nutrients: Great source of vitamin A, vitamin B12 and vitamin B6

Recipe: Hawaiian Chicken
Name: Monica Shaw
Original
  Calories 645
  Grams of Protein 41.5
  Grams of Carbohydrate 105.3
  Grams of Fat 4.9
  Fiber (grams) 3.3
  % calories from Protein 26
  % calories from Carbohydrate 67
  % calories from Fat 7
Special notes on nutrients: Great source of thiamin, niacin, and vitamin B6

Recipe: Honey Glazed Chicken
Name: Simona Soloveychik
Original
  Calories 303
  Grams of Protein 29
  Grams of Carbohydrate 39.8

Grams of Fat 3.1
Fiber (grams) —
Sodium (mg) 1445
% calories from Protein 38
% calories from Carbohydrate 53
% calories from Fat 9

Special notes on nutrients: Great source of niacin, and a good source of vitamin B6 and riboflavin (B2)

Recipe: Slow Cooker Chicken and Vegetables

Name: Kim Stiles

Original
Calories 423
Grams of Protein 32.4
Grams of Carbohydrate 41.1
Grams of Fat 15
Fiber (grams) 6.0
Sodium (mg) 798
% calories from Protein 30
% calories from Carbohydrate 38
% calories from Fat 32

Modified
Calories 352
Grams of Protein 31.9
Grams of Carbohydrate 33.3
Grams of Fat 10.4
Fiber (grams) 5.8
Sodium (mg) 492
% calories from Protein 36
% calories from Carbohydrate 38
% calories from Fat 26

Special notes on nutrients: Great source of vitamin A, niacin and vitamin B6

Recipe: Cabbage Chicken

Name: Kim Zmeskal

Original
Calories 387
Grams of Protein 35.2
Grams of Carbohydrate 45.3

Grams of Fat 5.9
Fiber (grams) 2.2
Sodium (mg) 1068
% calories from Protein 38
% calories from Carbohydrate 48
% calories from Fat 14
Special notes on nutrients: Great source of niacin, vitamin B6
and vitamin C

Recipe: Chicken Mozzarella
Name Kerri Strug
Original
Calories 375
Grams of Protein 51.3
Grams of Carbohydrate 23
Grams of Fat 8.6
Fiber (grams) .5
Sodium (mg) 1165
% calories from Protein 55
% calories from Carbohydrate 25
% calories from Fat 21
Special notes on nutrients: Great source of niacin, vitamin B6
and folate

CHAPTER 9

DESSERTS:
The Perfect Dismount

Fruit Pizza
Kim Arnold

Gymnastics Accomplishments:
-Israeli Peace Cup — 1st Vault, 1st Bars
-Marseilles Cup (France) — 2nd Vault, 3rd Floor, 4th All-Around
-4 time National Team Member

Quote: "I like this recipe because I like a lot of fruit and it's a healthy dessert, too."

Recipe received from: My grandmother

Recipe:
    1 package Pillsbury™ Sugar Cookie Dough
    2/3 tub Cool Whip™ (12 oz size)
    1/3 cup powdered sugar
    1/2 tsp vanilla
    1 pint strawberries
    2 bananas
    1 handful raspberries
    2 peaches
    1 small can mandarin oranges
    3 kiwi
    juice of 1 lemon

Slice and press the cookie dough into 1 large pizza pan (12"). Cook at 350° for 18-20 minutes. Let cool. Mix 2/3 tub of Cool Whip™ with 1/3 cup of powdered sugar and 1/2 tsp vanilla. Spread over cooled crust. Starting with the outer edge and working your way inward, put the slices of kiwi, then sliced strawberries, 1 small can of mandarin oranges, 2 bananas (mixed in lemon juice to prevent browning), 2 sliced peaches (also in lemon juice) and fill the center with raspberries. Cut into 8 slices. Note: Any other fruits may be substituted.

Yields: 8 slices

Tips from Michelle: Cut the fat by 6% by using Cool Whip™ Lite!

Sweet Potato Pie
Wendy Hilliard

Gymnastics Accomplishments:
-First black Rhythmic National Team member
-1984 Olympic Trials competitor
-3 time Rhythmic World Championships competitor

Quote: "It is the only thing I can bake. (It's a) family recipe (and) it tastes great."

Recipe received from: My sisters

Recipe:
 3 eggs
 1/2 cup sugar
 1/4 cup melted butter
 1/2 tsp salt
 1/3 cup evaporated milk
 1 tsp vanilla
 1 tsp cinnamon
 1 tsp nutmeg
 1-1/2 cups mashed sweet potatoes
 2 tbsp lemon juice
 1 unbaked pie shell

Preheat oven to 400 degrees. Beat eggs and sugar. Add melted butter, salt, milk and spices. Blend with potatoes and lemon juice. Pour into unbaked pie shell. Bake in oven for 10 minutes. Reduce heat to 300-350° and bake for another 35-40 minutes. Serve with whipped cream or plain. You can use canned sweet potatoes. If you're using fresh sweet potatoes, make sure to strain them.

Yields: 8 servings

Tips from Michelle: Here is where substituting applesauce for butter works well and the recipe still tastes great. A couple of other changes, and you can get rid of almost 11 grams of fat per slice!

Instead of:	Use:
1/4 cup butter	1/4 cup applesauce
1/3 cup evaporated milk	1/3 cup evaporated skim milk
unbaked pie shell	graham cracker pie shell

Baked Apples
Betty Okino

Gymnastics Accomplishments:
-1991 American Cup Champion
-1991, 1992 World Championship Medalist
-1992 Olympic Team — Bronze Medal (Team)

Quote: "I like the recipe, because I have a bad sweet tooth, and this recipe is a low calorie, great tasting and nutritious way to get rid of it."

Recipe received from: *Eat To Win*, by Dr. Robert Haas Δ

Recipe:

10 medium Rome apples
2-1/2 cups raisins
3 bananas
1-1/2 tsp allspice
2 tsp cinnamon
1 tsp arrowroot powder or
   cornstarch

1-1/2 cups orange juice
1-1/2 cups water
10 pitted prunes
6 tsp imitation brandy
   extract

Combine orange juice, water, cinnamon, allspice, cornstarch, and extract in a large saucepan. Bring to a boil, stirring constantly until sauce is slightly thickened. Preheat oven to 375 degrees. Core apples. Place in a baking dish and stuff center with raisins. Place rest of raisins in baking dish. Quarter prunes and lay around apples with raisins. Set aside 10 slices of banana. Place the rest around the apples. Pour juice mixture over apples. Pour some in the center of each apple. Top each apple core with a slice of banana. Bake 1 hour, basting every 15 minutes with liquid from dish. Cover while baking. Enjoy!

Yields: 10 servings

Δ Reprinted with permission

Fruit Smoothies
Traci Sommer

Gymnastics Accomplishments:
-1992 National Team Member/Olympic Trials competitor
-1992 Golden Sands, Bulgaria — 4th All-Around
-1991 American Classic — 1st All-Around

Quote: "(It) tastes good! A quick way to get in your fruits for the day as well as one serving of dairy."

Recipe received from: Mixed versions from various magazines

Recipe:
    3/4 cup sparkling water
    1/2 cup grapefruit juice
    2 peaches, sliced*
    1/2 ripe banana
    3/4 cup nonfat yogurt**
    1/2 tsp vanilla extract

Place all ingredients in blender in this order: 1/2 the fruits, then 1/2 the juices, then the rest of the fruits, then the rest of the juices. Blend until smoothies are thick. Once fruits begins to liquefy, check consistency frequently to be sure not to over whip. When finished, pour into glasses and enjoy.

Yields: 2 servings

* Peaches can also be replaced with any fruit in season, it's all up to your desired taste!

** Vanilla yogurt will work but any fruit flavored yogurt goes well also.

Chocolate Angelfood Cake
Lisa Wittwer Pitlick

Gymnastics Accomplishments:
-1983, 1984, 1985 National Team Member
-1983 Pan American Games Team — 1st Team, 3rd AA, 3rd Vault
   and Floor, 2nd Bars
-1988 Big Ten Conference — All-Around Champion

Quote: "I love angelfood cake, but I sometimes need the taste of chocolate and this cake definitely satisfies a chocolate craving. This cake doesn't need any frosting, it tastes great alone and on the run."

Recipe received from: Great Aunt Till

Recipe:
   1-1/2 cups sugar
   2/3 cup flour (sifted before measuring)
   1 tsp cream of tartar
   1-1/4 cups egg whites
   1/3 cup cocoa powder
   1/4 tsp salt
   1 tsp vanilla

Preheat oven to 325 degrees. Sift flour and cocoa together 3 times. Using a mixer, partially beat egg whites. Add cream of tartar and salt, then beat until stiff. Add sugar slowly, as well as vanilla. Stir in flour mixture. Pour into angelfood cake pan (ungreased). Using a knife, cut through the batter so there are no air bubbles. Bake for 1 hour.

Yields: 1 cake (about 8 servings)

Notes from Lisa: Tastes great with Cool Whip™ or frozen yogurt. It's a great dessert if a person needs a bit of chocolate but without the fat!

Lemon Whipped Cream Cake
Tim Daggett

Gymnastics Accomplishments:
-Scored a perfect 10.00 to clinch the gold medal for the 1984
    Olympic Team
-1984 Olympic Games Pommel Horse Bronze medalist
-Network broadcaster for the 1992 Olympic Games

Quote: "The whipped cream cake is very low in fat and delicious at the same time."

Recipe received from: Mom

Recipe:
    1 box angelfood cake mix
    1 box My-T-Fine™ lemon pie filling
    1-1/2 pints Cool Whip™ Lite

Bake angelfood cake as directed on box. Let cool. Make pie filling as directed on box. Fold in 1-1/2 pints Cool Whip™ Lite into pie filling. Horizontally cut cooled cake in half. Using a knife, make a 1-inch well around the cake for filling. Spoon in filling using a generous amount. Replace top of cake and cover remainder of cake with Cool Whip™ mixture. Refrigerate.

Yields: 8 slices

Note: Any lemon pie filling will work. Quantity should equal filling for one pie.

Frosted Chocolate Brownies
Pam Bileck

Gymnastics Accomplishments:
-1984 Olympic Team Member — Silver medal (Team)
-1984 National Beam Champion
-1983, 1985 World Championship Team Member

Quote: "I love dessert!"

Recipe received from: A friend

Recipe:
1/2 cup + 3 tbsp reduced calorie margarine, softened
1-1/3 cups sugar
8 egg whites
1/2 cup nonfat sour cream alternative
1/3 cup evaporated skim milk
2 tsp vanilla extract
1-1/3 cups all-purpose flour
1 tsp baking powder
1/2 tsp salt
2/3 cup unsweetened cocoa
Vegetable cooking spray
Creamy Chocolate Frosting*

Preheat oven to 350 degrees. Beat margarine at medium speed of an electric mixer until fluffy; gradually add sugar and beat well. Add egg whites, sour cream, milk, and vanilla; beat well. Combine flour and next three ingredients; stir well. Add flour mixture to creamed mixture, mixing well. Pour batter into 13" x 9" x 2" baking pan coated with cooking spray. Bake at 350° for 25 minutes or until a wooden pick inserted comes out clean. Cool in pan on a wire rack. Spread Creamy Chocolate Frosting over cooled brownies, and cut into squares.

*Creamy Chocolate Frosting

3 cups sifted powdered sugar
1/4 cup unsweetened cocoa
1/4 tsp salt
1/4 cup skim milk
1-1/2 tsp vanilla extract

Combine all ingredients in a medium bowl, stirring until frosting is of spreading consistency.

Yields: 24 brownies

Smoothie
Katie Teft

Gymnastics Accomplishments:
-1993 Level 10 National Champion
-1995 Pan American Team — 1st Team, 4th All-Around
-1995 U.S. Classic — 5th All-Around

Quote: "(I like this) because it's no fat and it tastes good."

Recipe:
3/4 pint strawberries
1/2 of a medium size banana, cut up
1-8 oz. container of nonfat, sugar free vanilla yogurt
4 ice cubes

Blend all ingredients in the blender on high speed for 1 minute.
Pour into 2 chilled glasses and serve.

Yield: 2 servings

Desserts Analysis
Per Serving

Recipe: Chocolate Angelfood Cake
Name: Lisa Wittwer Pitlick

Original
  Calories 219
  Grams of Protein 6.6
  Grams of Carbohydrate 47.4
  Grams of Fat .76
  Fiber (grams) —
  Sodium (mg) 176
  % calories from Protein 12
  % calories from Carbohydrate 85
  % calories from Fat 3
Special notes on nutrients: Good source of chocolate!!

Recipe: Baked Apples
Name: Betty Okino

Original
  Calories 261
  Grams of Protein 2.3
  Grams of Carbohydrate 67.5
  Grams of Fat 1.0
  Fiber (grams) 7.9
  Sodium (mg) 6.5
  % calories from Protein 3
  % calories from Carbohydrate 94
  % calories from Fat 3
Special notes on nutrients: Great source of fiber, vitamin C and a good source of vitamin B6

Recipe: Fruit Pizza
Name: Kim Arnold

Original
  Calories 337
  Grams of Protein 3.2
  Grams of Carbohydrate 54.1
  Grams of Fat 12.8

Fiber (grams) 4.8
Sodium (mg) 144
% calories from Protein 4
% calories from Carbohydrate 63
% calories from Fat 33

Modified
Calories 304
Grams of Protein 2.5
Grams of Carbohydrate 54.1
Grams of Fat 9.5
Fiber (grams) 4.8
Sodium (mg) 144
% calories from Protein 3
% calories from Carbohydrate 70
% calories from Fat 27

Special notes on nutrients: Great source of vitamin C and a good source of fiber.

Recipe: Sweet Potato Pie
Name: Wendy Hilliard

Original
Calories 293
Grams of Protein 4.8
Grams of Carbohydrate 28.6
Grams of Fat 19.1
Fiber (grams) —
Sodium (mg) 250
% calories from Protein 6
% calories from Carbohydrate 38
% calories from Fat 56

Modified
Calories 242
Grams of Protein 4.5
Grams of Carbohydrate 38.1
Grams of Fat 8.2
Fiber (grams) .08
Sodium (mg) 334
% calories from Protein 7
% calories from Carbohydrate 63
% calories from Fat 30

Special notes on nutrients: Good source of vitamin A

Recipe: Lemon Whipped Cream Cake
Name: Tim Daggett

Original
   Calories 387
   Grams of Protein 4.5
   Grams of Carbohydrate 77
   Grams of Fat 4.3
   Fiber (grams) —
   Sodium (mg) 450
   % calories from Protein 5
   % calories from Carbohydrate 84
   % calories from Fat 11

Recipe: Fruit Smoothies
Name: Traci Sommer

Original
   Calories 128
   Grams of Protein 5.4
   Grams of Carbohydrate 27.9
   Grams of Fat 0.3
   Fiber (grams) 2.8
   Sodium (mg) 61
   % calories from Protein 16
   % calories from Carbohydrate 82
   % calories from Fat 2

Special notes on nutrients: Great vitamin C source

Recipe: Chocolate Frosted Brownies
Name: Pam Bileck

Original
   Calories 170
   Grams of Protein 2.8
   Grams of Carbohydrate 33.7
   Grams of Fat 3.5
   Fiber (grams) —
   Sodium (mg) 163
   % calories from Protein 6
   % calories from Carbohydrate 76
   % calories from Fat 18

Recipe: Smoothie
Name: Katie Teft

Original
- Calories 115
- Grams of Protein 6.5
- Grams of Carbohydrate 22.6
- Grams of Fat .60
- Fiber (grams) 3.0
- Sodium (mg) 82
- % calories from Protein 21
- % calories from Carbohydrate 74
- % calories from Fat 5